DIARY OF A TRAMP

Also by John D. Vose:

LADY OF CONNEMARA
YOUR FEET ARE KILLING ME!
CLERICAL CAPERS

DIARY OF A TRAMP
John D. Vose

UNITED WRITERS
Cornwall

UNITED WRITERS PUBLICATIONS LTD
Trevail Mill, Zennor, St. Ives, Cornwall.

All rights Reserved. No part of this publication may be reproduced, stored in a retrieval system, or transmitted, in any form or by any means, electronic, mechanical, photocopying, recording or otherwise, without the prior permission of the Copyright owner.

ISBN 901976 70 9

Copyright (c) John D. Vose 1981

Printed in Great Britain by
United Writers Publications Ltd
Cornwall

This book is dedicated
to all those who do not
follow the herd and
have the courage to be
'different'.

CONTENTS

Chapter		Page
1	Early Days	9
2	The Spike	18
3	Bloody Mary's	30
4	Grim Times	40
5	The Road Beckons	52
6	Kirkby Lonsdale	65
7	Singing and Poaching	80
8	On the Way to the Lakes	94
9	The Lakes	109
10	Summer Bumming	124
11	Knuttles of Navan	138
12	More Ways of Making a Living	152
13	Christmas Day in the Doss-house	170
14	A Winter's Tale	179
15	Terminus	194

1

EARLY DAYS

During my days as a tramp I travelled many roads and met many people. Whether my life will be found to be exciting and interesting, the popular ingredients of a man's own story, I cannot rightly say, I enjoyed my days on the road and at least I can claim that my tale is somewhat different. A story, like the road, has a beginning and an end and for that beginning let me take you to a pretty Cheshire village in the year 1900. I am, as far as I know, the only tramp to be born there so I will not bring dishonour on it by naming it, or upon the name of my family for my father's sake. The title 'tramp' had a terrible stigma associated with it, and equal with such words as 'workhouse', 'soup kitchen' and 'charity', yet there is a fascination about the past despite the grimness, and in these pages I hope I have painted a pen-picture of life for a man on the road between the two wars 1918 – 1939.

My first recollection of my mother is of a tall, blonde-haired woman with blazing eyes. Mother's eyes always seemed to be blazing and were kept company by her tongue, which never seemed to lie in peace in her head. I am sure my birth must have been a dreadful torment to my mother for she certainly seemed to spend most of her time in taking her spite out on me.

Whatever I did as a child in her eyes was wrong. She screeched and ranted and constantly rowed with my father. I have little doubt that they had rowed from the hour of my birth, on a cold December afternoon in 1900, and I don't doubt they had rowed from the very day they had married. Such is the memory of my mother. But just as this is a sour one, the memory of my father is a happy one. I will never forget his love of the countryside and how we would go for walks together — never with my mother — and how we would chase each other through the tall grass and count out loud the tolls of the village church bell; there was a five-barred gate on which I would perch myself, clinging leech-like to the top, whilst my father pushed the gate backwards and forwards, there was laughter in his voice and kindness in his face, a friend to everyone we met and a man for whom Nature held the very reason for his being alive.

And then the war came and he was one of the first men in our village to enlist of his own free will. I was fifteen at the time and felt proud of my father going to war to fight for his country and yet I was sad, for I had a sense of foreboding about his going; my mother did not seem to care, there were no tears on her face like there were on the face of Mrs Brogden, our neighbour, whose husband had also enlisted. She cried openly in the street and I felt a great sadness at the shattering effect of war on a sleepy, peaceful village.

Where dad fought in the war I do not remember now, but he wrote home regularly. Mother never spoke of him and to me he was gone, as it were, for ever.

And then began a procession of men to the cottage, strangers I had not seen before. I didn't know it at the time, for I had led a very sheltered existence being mainly in my father's company, that my mother was a prostitute. She became the talk of the village but she didn't care. I was taunted and jibed and one day I fought a lad who had shouted obscenities about her as we played cricket on the village patch. My face was like a piece of raw beef when I got home and for my troubles I received a swipe across the face from the woman whose character I had tried to defend.

After school I had found work as a farmhand on an estate several miles walk from the village. Dad had always encouraged me to study, for he was something of a literary man being a composer of witty, entertaining poetry which he would read to me when mother was out of the cottage, for she considered poetry to be a pastime for idiots and people with their heads in the clouds. After a few months on the farm the squire asked me if I would like to work in the Estate Office. I liked the young squire and he had often good-naturedly jibed me upon my fondness of reading books during my dinner break.

"What are you stuffing your head with today, young Joe?" he would shout from his pony and trap.

But my love of reading had obviously swayed him when he was looking for an assistant clerk in the Estate Office. Life was meaningful and I enjoyed the work. The squire paid me handsomely enough and fed me well, but then he went to the war himself and his brother took over the running of the estate. I had always disliked his brother and set out never to cross him, which I never did, but somehow my heart was no longer in the job, even though the agent, Mr Jeffry, was a good enough fellow to work for.

Meanwhile, my father wrote to me and I replied, but whether or not he received the letters I never discovered. He came home exactly two weeks before the war was officially declared to be at an end, a broken shell-shocked man whose hands shook like branches of a tree in a high wind. He didn't seem to know me, there was a sadness in his eyes and he would sit for hours on end with his head buried in his hands. At night he would shout and then mother announced one morning that she could stand it no longer. She left and I saw no more of her or heard anything about her whereabouts.

Dad's condition grew worse. Mr Jeffry, the agent, would give me days off to stay with my father. The hours were filled with deep depressions, relieved only by bouts of bawling which would end in wailing and tears. The squire, my original employer, had been killed in action and now his younger brother had the full run of the estate. He constantly accused Mr Jeffry of not managing the estate properly, and when he heard that I was being given days off work to look after my father he grew angry. He warned me that if I did it again I would lose my job. Dad was pathetic by this time and I had no option but to stay at home with him. Shortly, a messenger lad came to the house with a letter of dismissal from the estate.

A week later two well-dressed official-looking men came to the cottage. They were detectives. They told me that my father was an Army deserter and that if he had been caught by the Army before he had reached England he would have been shot. As it was, he would receive not a brass farthing and I would hear more of the matter. I pleaded with them that my father was very sick and told them how he had enlisted in the Army voluntarily.

One of them thawed slightly as they left and said "We'll see, son, we'll see."

A month later a van came to the cottage. A man in a black suit, carrying a doctor's bag, came in to see dad. After an examination he told me that, unless I could trace my mother and that she would agree to look after him, there was no alternative but to take him to an asylum.

"The war affected many men," he told me, and there was warmth in his words and in his eyes. "No, he was not a coward, your father," he said, anticipating the question burning in my innards. "He is a sick man, he cannot stay here."

They took him away that very day and there was no recognition in his eyes as I fondled his hands in farewell. "You've done your best, lad," said the doctor and off the van went, down the lane and passed the favourite haunts of my childhood when dad was in his prime.

I was out of work and as the cottage belonged to the estate I could no longer afford to continue to pay the rent, though I had some money saved, a few meagre pounds, and I determined I would cling to what was left once I had paid the rent we owed on the cottage. Eviction would be the next step because, with the men returning from the war, there was a housing shortage and the squire made it quite clear he wanted to put a new farm manager into our cottage.

Finding employment in the vicinity of the village was like searching for jewels in a dung heap, just as hopeless. The only solution was to leave the village. Work could be found in a big town or city, surely? I was naive enough to believe this as I set out with just the clothes I stood up in, some cheese and bread in an ancient haversack, along with a clean shirt, a change of underclothes and the few pounds wrapped up in a muslin bag buried beneath the clothes in the bottom of the sack.

My first two days were spent foot-slogging and sleeping rough at night, subsisting on the bread and cheese I had taken with me. On the third day I arrived in Liverpool. I was a fit lad and the two days spent walking hadn't had any adverse effect on me in any way. In fact, I felt elated by the adventure of it, the hopes of the young were burning brightly inside me and I felt that I was starting out on a new and interesting life, simply exchanging the country for the city. My first need was somewhere to sleep whilst I looked for work. Close to the docks, I found a lodging house for working men, a totally different establishment to the common lodging houses of which I was to learn so much about later. We slept five in a room. I had a single bed, but four men shared a double bed. For breakfast we got tea and toast, sometimes with margarine and sometimes with dripping, and the evening meal was invariably a watered-down version of Liverpool's notorious lob scouse. For this I paid the sum of two shillings and sixpence each day and did without food during the rest of the day whilst looking for work.

I tried all the offices I could find. I must have walked scores of miles up flights of stairs alone, but always I had to descend without employment. The clerks who had gone to the war had returned, during the hostilities young ones had been taken on, now many of these had lost their jobs and were in a similar plight to my own. For hours I combed the streets of the city and when I had exhausted the city centre I tried the dock area and the shipping firms. It was always the same – NO WORK. I was young, strong and healthy so I decided to ask at every warehouse, wharf and dock if there was some sort of manual work available. The tremendous influx back from the Armed Services had done the same at the docks. The work force was now completely full and any jobs that had been vacant were immediately filled by the men nearing retirement age. I joined queues of old men waiting at the gates for the chance of a day's work, slouching dispirited men who had been forced into early retirement to make way for the returning heroes. Men who, at their age, would never be in full employment again. The nearest I got to even being considered was a rough appraisal from a stevedore's foreman, who said: "You'd not last five minutes here, kid. You look like a pen-pusher to me. Tried the warehouses?" I took his advice. But every shipping office, every cabin which seemed to contain clerkish work, was full up.

After a fortnight I was realising that my dreams of security and work were a myth. The war was over, thousands of men had returned, still more were returning daily. What chance had I, an outsider from the country, got of work in a city?

The lodging house was no longer feasible. I had a few shillings left and now I was beginning to discover the whereabouts of the free handouts in the city. The stall run by some charitable organisation whose name I forget; the dockland soup kitchen run by the Salvation Army; the 'prayer and a bun' tin hut where you got a sermon lasting an hour and a cup of tea and a bun at the end of it. At first I hadn't the courage to take charity, but a rumbling stomach, sharp with hunger pangs, soon knocks the stupid pride from a man. So this became my pattern: charity during the day as I still kept on slogging the streets in search of work, and a common lodging house at night where you provided your own food and cooked it on a communal stove. I rationed myself to two-pen'arth of meat, which I bought from a back-street scrag-end butcher who sold the very poorest and cheapest of meat. For the rest, I filled myself upon tea which I found on the docks, showered down when the tea crates were smacked against a warehouse wall by the jolting of the unloading cranes. My pockets were always full of it and at the lodging house I became known as 'the Chinaman' because the tea was the best blend of China it was possible to obtain, and in return for this luxury I was given scraps by the other men to go with my two pennyworth of scrag-end in the pan. But more of these common lodging houses later, for these places almost warrant a book to themselves.

One of the 'regulars' in the doss-house was a chap by the name of Clive, who was constantly ribbed by the other men because of his name. He was a clerk who had fallen on bad times due to drink. He reeked of the stuff, but he retained a certain dignity which, in his sober periods, was directed to me. He hated himself for the way he had fallen.

"Disgusting swine this lot," he would say. "You must get out of this, lad. Oh! I know you try, but once the lodging-house circuit starts, boy, it's the devil's own job to break it."

It could almost have been a clergyman speaking. I was not fully aware of his meaning then but later on I realised the stark truth of his words and the bitter, unvarnished accuracy of them. His eyes were blood-shot and water constantly dribbled down his cheeks. But, somehow, his short-cropped ginger military-like moustache and the faded red cravat gave him a shabby-genteel appearance of authority and even a vestige of respectability.

It was Clive who provided me with a lead for a job. He had seen a notice on an Employment Office Board stating that a Ships Chandler's office required a clerk. Applicants to apply in their own handwriting the notice stated. Clive produced a sheet of paper and an envelope, along with a pot of ink and a pen. Noticing the look on my face, he said: "Yes, I stole it from the porter's desk at the Adelphi Hotel. I hardly think they will go out of business through it. Now wash your hands, boy, and write. I will check the letter over."

When my application was completed he read the letter eagerly. "Excellent! You have a neat, tidy hand. The English is good, straight to the point. The letter has the smack of education. I have been a Head Clerk in a large office, boy, and I know the value to the applicant of a well written letter. Let us hope that the number of the house and the street won't give the game away that you are the resident of a common lodging-house. And now, boy, there only remains the stamp — also stolen. Now, here, post it. Immediately, now!"

In return for his kindness, even though he had stolen to help me, for my narrow-minded christian principles were still untarnished then, I gave him a cupful of tea leaves which would keep Clive going through the 'dry' hours when he had nothing stronger to befuddle his once acute and efficient mind.

Three days later a typed letter arrived from the Company Secretary, a Mr Blackstone, asking me to attend for an interview on the following morning at 10 o'clock. The office was in a side street off Dale Street. Clive had been as elated as I was about the interview and had spent a whole hour rubbing at my boots with newspaper in an attempt to give them some sort of respectable appearance. My once neat suit of clothes was badly crumpled and soiled, but it was all I had. At least I was clean, for the night before I scrubbed myself down with an old loofah I had found in a back entry and a block of harsh green soap someone gave me in exchange for a pocketful of tea.

Clive accompanied me to the building and shook my hand before I went inside. "Best of luck, Chinaman."

Mr Blackstone was a small, portly man in a black suit, unrelieved in any way by splashes of colour. On his stubby nose perched a pair of pince-nez which he looked over rather than through. I bade him 'Good morning, sir' but there was no reply. He simply stared at me before waving me to a chair. But even in that wave I noticed a hesitancy in case I should spoil his office chair.

"You wrote this letter?" There was surprise in his question.

"I did, sir. I trust it is to your liking."

"Oh, indeed — indeed. But I must say, young man, that your appearance gives a lie to the letter."

"If you wish, sir, then I will write a sample letter for you here and now, sir," I said.

"Oh, I don't doubt you wrote it. It's simply that I do not condone the conduct of an applicant who comes for an interview dressed as you are dressed. You are down-at-heel, sir, and the suit would be more fitting to a scarecrow." He had risen to his feet and was surveying me with a critical eye. The man was sneering and I began to grow angry inside, but I knew that to do so would mean disaster. Instead, I tried to reason with him. To be truthful was my only chance so I told him of my experience as a clerk in the Estate Office and how I had been forced to leave Cheshire to look for work in Liverpool. But all he said was: "So you admit to being sacked? You have no references." He had completely ignored the genuine hard-luck element of my story. "How can I, as the Company Secretary of a reputed firm of Ships Chandlers, take on a clerk who is dressed like a tramp? What would a ship's captain think if the representative of B— and H— came aboard his ship looking like you do? What do you say to that, boy?" The man had autocracy written into every line and wrinkle of his face.

"Only that if you give me a chance, sir, I will soon have a new suit of clothes and I will prove to you that I am a competent clerk and a respectable young man." I was pleading with him now, not in the words I used, but in my tone of voice. Above his head, over the chair on which he now sat, was a religious tract urging the sinner to repent.

With a sanctimonious sniff, he said, "Ugh! money in advance, is it? New clothes? No, sir, we are not a firm of philanthropists. If you attend for interview you attend in the attire one expects of the holder of the post for which you have applied."

"But in my circumstances, how do I find suitable clothes?" It seemed a reasonable question.

"That, young man, is your affair. You got yourself into the state you are in, don't make excuses for yourself, so it is up to you to get yourself out of it. Good morning to you." The interview was at an end.

I glanced once more at the impassive face, the gold pince-nez, and the tract above his head. This man worshipped the God I worshipped. I found it strange that here was a man who exhibited the words of the Bible on his wall yet turned a cold heart to one who asked him for a chance to earn a decent living. I was a young fool in those days and hadn't yet learned that many so-called religious people are nothing but canting hypocrites. It is so easy to be moral on a full stomach. I simply said, "Good morning, sir," and left the office. At least I had preserved my politeness.

Clive was waiting for me outside and when I told him what had passed he said it all for me. Raising his fist he shook it passionately at the high building and screeched. "You sanctimonious son of a bastard" and, with that, he sat down on the front step of the building and drank from a bottle of methylated spirits. I whispered a word of thanks in his ear and went on my way, determined to leave Liverpool once and for all.

2

THE SPIKE

My way now was North for I had heard that there was an asylum in a village called Rainhill situated roughly half way between Liverpool and Warrington. I had nowhere particular to go anyway so I reasoned that it was possible my father could be an inmate there. I reached the hospital in the late afternoon and on mentioning my father's name at the office I was told that he was indeed a patient.

A doctor spoke to me. "You'd better know, young man, that your father can be very violent. There are times when we have to restrain him and keep him in a padded cell. I'm afraid he won't know you."

I wish now that I had not seen him for the memory I took away with me was a horrid one, of a man who had become a lunatic. And yet I felt it was my duty to search for his whereabouts. He had only stared at me vacantly when I sat before him on a chair. After a few minutes a nurse advised me to leave. The doctor who had spoken to me earlier assured me that there was nothing that could be done for dad, he wasn't suffering, the war had produced many men like him who were now cabbages as far as their mental powers were concerned. The doctor promised that dad would be well looked after and he shook my hand as I left the ward. At least I felt I had met a compassionate, caring man and I took some comfort from my chat with him.

By this time I had exactly fourpence in my pocket and upon enquiring of a policeman if there was anyone in the area who would give a man food and lodging in return for a few hours work, he shook his head. "Your best bet is the spike at Whiston. About a mile and a half back in the direction of Liverpool."

I reached it by way of a path across ploughed fields. I had never heard the word spike before, but soon found it to be the popular name given to the casual ward of a workhouse. These spikes have always been detested by the 'seasoned' tramps, they represented the coldest side of the coin of charity, the sinking to the lowest depths for a man who only went there out of sheer desperation. I was to find out later that these places usually had a line of men outside them, queueing to get a bed for the night. The time on the workhouse clock stood at 6.15 p.m. The entrance to the casual ward was through a long, dark passage and, even though the evening was warm for November, I felt a shivery feeling as I walked towards a wooden hut in which a single window was framed. A florid faced, fat man glared at me as I tapped on the glass. From the look on his face you would have imagined that I was an unrepentant sinner trying to wangle my way through the gates of Heaven. He slid open the hatch in the window and, pushing his head through the aperture, looked me up and down suspiciously.

"Yer late ain't yar? Only a kid aint yar? Want a bed does yar?" He was answering his own questions as he fumbled with a huge red leather-bound ledger that looked like the Book of Ages.

"I'm sorry if I'm late. I was sent by a policeman." I tried to sound apologetic for I had nowhere else to sleep for the night if he refused me. Mention of the policeman helped me.

"Sent by the law was yar?" He looked at me hard for a few seconds. "Well listen, mate, in view of yar age I'll let yer in but think on, my lad, that if yar come here in future yar comes for six and no later − savvy? Nar, I wants a few partic'lars I does − name?"

"Joseph Simpson," I lied, for I felt ashamed to give my own name.

"Yar sure nar, ain't yar? It's an offence to give yar wrong name in a casual ward."

I looked him squarely in the face and gave him a lying nod. That was two lies.

"Any property?"

"No."

"Any money?" This time I was truthful. I placed the four pence on the small counter. The fat man's eyes watered as he laughed: "We've got bleedin' Rothschild 'onouring us with his company we 'as." He gave a huge belly laugh that shook him like a jelly. "Where yar come from?" he resumed, all officious once again.

"Liverpool."

"Where yar 'eadin'? Which tarn?" His voice was a most peculiar mixture of cockney and Liverpool.

"Manchester," I said, simply because I knew that Manchester lay vaguely ahead somewhere in a rough northerly direction.

Pen poised in mid air, he looked at me hard and said slowly. "Nar look here, cock. I wants a proper answer. What yar up to anyway? Yar a novice ain't yar? How old are yar?"

"Nineteen, sir, almost twenty," I replied. He looked up sharply at the 'sir'. He obviously liked it. Despite his roughness there was kindness about the man.

"Yar ain't used ta this life are yar, son? No, well see when a spike officer asks yar where yars going yar says the next spike in the opposite direction to where you've come from. Savvy?"

I nodded though I certainly didn't understand what he was talking about. I was in a fantasy world armed with the knowledge that very soon I was to come well and truly down to earth.

"I reckon as I'll put you in with Teddy Bear. Yar'l like old Teddy Bear, loves to yarn and tell the young 'uns all about it does Teddy. This way, lad." I followed him into the casual ward proper which was an extension building of the workhouse itself and gave the impression of being added on as an after-thought.

And so I entered my first spike and received my first lesson in the strange and diabolical workings of these places which the government seemed to think beneficial to the down-and-out on the road. In fact, they served the very opposite purpose, were an affront to the dignity of manhood, and I thank God that I have not had to spend many nights in them; for the seasoned tramp, the man who had made up his mind that the road was his way of life, despised these cess pits of bureaucracy where they kept you barely alive as a balm to their consciences, because England is a Christian country and it would be the act of barbarians to deny men a roof over their heads and a crust of bread and margarine.

But there, I am off on my favourite topic like a politician carried away with the vocal diarrhoea of his calling. The spikes represented home to thousands of men and women who preferred to keep on the move than live in the workhouse — the House of Shame to thousands of folk who lived their lives just one step above it, dreading that the day would dawn when they would be compelled to enter the workhouse gates and live the confined life of a pauper in a suit of workhouse grey.

The thought of the workhouse made me shudder as the fat man led me across a bare concrete room then down a passage, heavy with the fetid smell of sweat, veiled by carbolic and that heavy reek of charity and pauperism that haunted every institution in the land, and a nauseating cocktail it made. He led me into the wash-house where three men were in the process of scrubbing themselves, whilst another was soaking in a zinc tub. The floor was a pool of black-brown scum.

"Strip off," ordered the fat man, but kindly. "Then leave yar clothes 'ere and tie 'em up with this cord, see. And I'd take yar fourpence with yar if I was you, cock. Nar when yar've done hop into that tub over yonder. It's too late for clean water, anyway it's only been used twice. And when yar've done get into this." He handed me a long, grey sacking smock that looked as if it and soap and water were the deadliest of enemies. It smelled of sweaty bodies.

"It's dirty," I protested with the innocence of an Oliver Twist.

"Effing dirty is it? Giving trouble is he, Dick? What's 'e think 'e is, a bleedin' Dook?" It was a thin weasil-faced man who swore so foully. He was the tramp-major I found out later, a man one step up from a tramp, usually an ex-tramp and often a creep or a nark to the police, given a permanent lodging place in the workhouse where he acted as an overseer to the casuals. Like a lot more members of our human race, he represented the old, ageless story of the man who is given a little authority, the stuff dictators are made of. I have met decent tramp-majors, but the vast majority have been of the other sort. I immediately mentally catalogued this one as a bully.

"E's OK Fred," said Fat Dick. "E's new on the road. E's got fourpence, by the way." He was imparting knowledge of importance, though I didn't know it. This news of money brought a gleam to the tramp-major's eyes. "Has 'e?" Was all he said. Then added "What's 'e in?" "Number Four," came the answer.

The thin man wrote something in a grubby notebook with a stub of pencil which he kept perched behind an ear while I made a mental note that the fourpence and I would not be parted without a struggle. What I didn't know then was that it was an offence to take money into a spike, but officials sometimes turned a blind eye so they could sell tea to the men with money.

The water had left an oily scum on my body and I felt dirtier after the bath than I did before, and after I had made a charade of drying myself on a sopping wet towel, gave up the idea and, wrapping myself in the dirty garment, made my way along a narrow corridor to find number four. I found it and opened the door nervously. "Welcome, mate," came a warm greeting. The speaker was an old decrepit-looking chap who looked as if he had stepped out of the pages of a history book; frail, with deep sunken eyes in a gaunt face, his whole appearance was one of a man who, for countless years, had existed just barely above the starvation level.

"I'm Teddy Bear," he announced. As he had white curly hair and a scrubby white beard to match, little of his face was visible. "Spare kip over yonder." He indicated a hammock-like affair supported by chains which were secured into the brickwork of the wall to give it suspension. There was one thick blanket of the same drab hue as the smock I was wearing.

I looked around, still nervous. But even over-riding the feeling of nervousness was a deep sense of shame. There were five other men in the cell, for it couldn't be given the title of 'room'. There was no covering of any description, either on the walls or the floor, simply bricks and concrete, cell-like and cold. At one end stood a large pot which was the communal latrine. I could almost feel every eye in that cell following my startled glances.

"Not the bloody Ritz, is it, cock?" said a red-haired lank fellow lying on the hammock next to mine. "And don't rock or you'll fall on your bloody face," he advised as I contrived to climb into the thing.

Then there was a clanging noise in the passage. "Dinner is served!" I recognised the voice of the fat man. He knocked the door open with his fat posterior and dragged in an iron trolley containing steaming cups of tea. He handed us a cup apiece, then a tin plate each containing two slices of bread and margarine. This was the casual ward evening meal eaten by tens of thousands of men and boys throughout the land. The tea was very good, but the grub tasted foul — but at least it was food, or a poor excuse for it. The fat man gave us a good-natured "Good-night" and left.

"You're a newcomer, you are," said Teddy Bear in a deliberate statement of cold fact. "I can tell a new lad a mile off. I'm on me last legs and the rest of these poor beggars are on the road some years, ain't you, lads?"

There was a pause as the men munched greedily and noisily at the bread and marge. Then a voice said: "you speak for your bleedin' self, old man." The speaker was a tall, gangling black-haired fellow with a stubble on his chin that looked capable of shredding a lump of stone. I took an immediate dislike to the man.

"No need to get ratty, Bert," said Teddy Bear. There was a distinct trace of education in the old man's voice.

"Well, just you remember as I fought in the bleedin' war. You lot might be bleedin' tramps, but I ain't, see? Fought for bloody king and soddin' country. Land fit for bloody heroes they promised us what lived like rats in the soddin' trenches and here I am living like a stinking rat with no piggin' work and no bleedin' chance of any. Call this a bloody fair country? Bleedin' dictatorship's more like it! It's this shaggin' government, I tell you, and that sod Lady bloody Astor, a bleedin' woman M.P. Women may be alright in bed, but they're no bloody use any other bleedin' place." Almost every other word was an expletive.

"I agree with you, Bert," said Teddy Bear. "But don't blame Lady Astor. She's the first woman M.P., yes, but she's hardly to blame for your plight and the plight of thousands of others, don't forget that. It's the system that's wrong. No individual is greater than the system."

"Aye, the effin' system." growled Bert, running his index finger down the inside of the mug to extract the last drop of moisture. He sucked it greedily. Teddy Bear continued:

"The system is to blame for us. Instead of trying to be constructive over the problem of homeless men it buries its head in the sands of complacency and bureaucracy."

"Aye the pissing system sends you to fight for the country then it doesn't want to know. You call it the frigging system, well I call it the greed of the bastard aristocrats and politicians; smarmy lot of bastards the bleedin' lot I says. Feather their own bleedin' nests and shag the rest of us. I'm alright but eff you. Jack! That's their motto." And so on and so on . . .

I was to find later this hatred of aristocracy and politicians typical of the way men on the road thought. To them the world was divided into two: the 'have's' and the 'have-nots'. But in their eyes the first had everything it is possible for a rich man to have, while the latter had nothing. There was no middle road. And the system was always the oppressor. To me it seemed ludicrous that seven grown men should be lying in bed at seven o'clock in the evening.

The talk continued in this vein for well over an hour, with Bert's nauseating, filthy language holding sway over opinions expressed by any of the others. The man disgusted me and as much as I tried to understand that he, like my own father, had fought in the war in conditions said to be the worst in any war, I couldn't blame an employer for refusing such a man a job. He was of the habitual belly-aching breed of tramps, and he was already a tramp whether he owned to the title or not, and would never be anything else. It is impossible for a human being to be completely without pride.

After what must have been a spell of almost two hours

the door opened and this time Fred, the tramp-major, stood before us bearing a tray full of steaming mugs of tea. The smell of tea was glorious to my nostrils.

"Who wants a cup? Penny each." There was a cunning look about the scoundrel. He was a creep of the worst kind.

'We ain't got no bleedin' money and you knows it," said Bert. "You bloody searched us yourself. Piss off!" He looked at me because he knew I had fourpence. *You* want a cup?" He leered.

"It's a half-penny a cup and you know it," said old Teddy Bear indignantly.

"It's gone up," said Fred with that ferret-like leer on his face.

"I'll give you fourpence for seven cups. A cup each," I offered.

Fred gave me a thin-lipped toothless grin. "Will you now? A penny a cup, I said, and that's it. You ain't in no position to bargain, mate. You wants tea, then you pays for it."

"Well, you can keep it," I said, even though I was dying for a hot drink to warm my shaking guts.

Fred knew when he was beaten and he placed the tray down on the floor with a rattle. "Then pick it up yourselves. I ain't no nursemaid."

I handed over the fourpence, which I had been holding in a clenched fist. He swore and snatched it from my hand.

"You've made a handsome bleedin' profit now, so piss off," said Bert. "To think I fought for that idle swine."

It was obvious that the weasel-looking tramp-major was frightened of Bert for he scarpered quickly. Not that I blamed him for that.

"Thanks, lad," said Teddy Bear politely, and they all thanked me in turn except Bert. He took it for his right. Perhaps, in his twisted way, he took me for a government spy. "And now," said Teddy Bear, after taking one long, soothing swig at the tea, "I'm going to tell this young lad here about the spikes. I'm an old hand and I reckon that I owe him an explanation."

And so on my very first night in a casual ward the mysteries of the spikes were opened up to me by the likeable old man who spoke with profound knowledge of a subject he knew from A to Z, and to which his emaciated body gave amen.

It was a bitter damp day which greeted us in the workhouse yard the next morning. A clock told me that it was seven o'clock. I was dressed once more in my own clothes, but they seemed to have little protection against the raw morning air which bit at my feet and legs and numbed my fingers. I had slept in spasms, but the periods of wakefulness had been long ones for it wasn't possible to sleep all night in a spike. In every communal room there was always a man with a consumptive cough and the procession to the latrine was a constant one.

Fred, the tramp-major, was on yard duty, dressed in a heavy, warm-looking coat.

"Pinched that coat off a bloke, he did," a voice in my ear informed me.

Trunks of trees cut up into varying lengths littered the yard, which was cobbled. "I don't know what they do with the wood because they don't heat the bleedin' spike with it," said the same voice.

"It all goes to the workhouse, ruddy sight warmer in there," someone else said, a shudder in the voice.

"Right, get sawing and cutting," ordered Fred, indicating a pile of axes and saws. The breath of the inmates rose like white vapour in the air. "The sooner you gets it done the sooner you gets your breakfast. Come on, Old Father Time, stop shaking like a blushing bride and pick up an axe."

This last remark was addressed to Teddy Bear. The old man was badly affected by the cold and his hands wouldn't grip on the handle of the axe. They were blue and the end of one finger had a blackish look.

"Pick the blasted thing up!" taunted Fred.

"It's no use," said Teddy Bear," my hands won't work. They've pained me all night."

"Then it's warming up they want, isn't it, old man, get your blood moving, won't it? You do no bloody work and you gets no bloody breakfast. Remember you're a bloody casual and unless you obeys the rules you gets no grub, see? You knows the law and I'm here to see it's carried out."

The rest of us were sawing and cutting eagerly for it was either that or freeze, but old Teddy Bear was bent over like a scarecrow figure crying into his beard.

"Right, it's the bloody house for you," shouted Fred. The 'house' meant the workhouse.

"I'm not going in there. Look, have a heart and give me a mug of tea and I'll do my work afterwards. I promise I'll do my share." The old man was pleading. "Then let me warm my hands."

"Not ruddy likely. Rules is rules. I reckon as you ain't fit to be on the road, old 'un, not no more. I've heard tales as you's cracking up quickly. You'll not last another winter, mate. You go into the main building, mate. You're an 'as-been. Look after yer well in the house." His voice was cruelly sarcastic. I could see from the expressions on the faces of many of the men that they were sorely tempted to strike Fred.

Now, in actual fact, it was not uncommon for old sick tramps to be advised to go into the body of the workhouse and to give up their life on the road. This was often genuine compassionate advice given by kindly officials, but Fred knew Teddy Bear's detestation of the 'house' for, like many old tramps, he firmly believed that it was the next step to the grave, a sort of knacker's yard where old men of the road were quietly disposed of. Fred knew this fear only too well and loved to taunt and tantalise the old timers like Teddy Bear.

"I'm not going in no bloody house," said the old man firmly. It was the first time I had heard him swear.

"Don't you swear at me, white whiskers. I'm your superior, get it?"

"You're a bleedin' swine, that's what you are." It was my nauseating comrade of the cell, Bert, who had spoken. Many another man would have attacked him for it, but not Fred. Instead, he took his rage out on old Teddy Bear. With his right fist clenched, he lashed out at the old man and, for all the tramp-major's spindly frame, there was frustrated rage in the blow which would surely have knocked the old man to the ground on to a pile of stones behind him. But the blow never landed for I kicked his legs from under him with a vicious lash of my right foot. He crumpled to the cobbled yard with a groan of agony. He thrust his hand upwards and we saw fingers twisted and contorted like knobbly twigs. He slowly rose to his feet.

"You've broken my bloody fingers!" he yelled and, picking up a stone with his free hand, he flung it at my face. Ducking, I struck him with my fist under the jaw and down he went to measure his length on the cobbled stones. Blood oozed from the back of his head.

"You'd better scarper now, mate!" yelled a voice.

"No good, the gates are locked," shouted another.

"Then get him on the roof – the roof!"

"Aye the roof – the roof!" Many voices had taken up the cry now. "Shoulders – up with him – the roof – the roof!" There was a mêlée of men all around me and I was hoisted by many hands until I stood on the tallest man's shoulders. "Now leap for the ledge and below yer's freedom, mate. Be smart, mate," he urged.

I was smart all right. Fear and the realisation that I might have killed a tramp-major possessed me with a terrible desire to take flight. From the ledge of the washhouse roof to the passage below was a drop of quite eight feet, but I didn't hesitate and found myself outside the building and only a few yards from the main road. I could hear Fat Dick's voice now and I heard another voice say, "He's out cold and no mistake." I ran down that road as if a whole army of demon bats were after me, out to suck my life blood – on I ran, mile after mile, staggering, falling, but still pressing on in a feverish dash for I knew not where. No hand was placed on my shoulder. I was not apprehended and as the time approached the hour of the mid-day break for those lucky enough to be in work, my fear gave way to hunger. I had no idea where I was. I knew I had travelled a long way from Whiston, but to the police the distance I had travelled would be nothing. If I had killed the man then I was a murderer; the thought rang in my brain like the clang of a great bell and I could see the rope before me and, once more, my fear took over as the over-riding passion and killed the gnawing hunger in my guts. In a blind panic, with the afternoon grey and drawing on to evening, I collapsed by the side of a bridge which carried the road over a canal. Below me I heard men talking. They were bargees, sitting on the towpath eating a meal. I was sorely tempted to ask them for food but I was too frightened to do so. I was so afraid that I thought every man, woman and child in the country would know that there was a man on the run. I just lay in a hollow hidden from the road, and when I felt refreshed I continued on my way.

After a mile or so I saw a milestone which said Manchester 3 miles. There would be lodging-houses there, it was a large city where a man could hide. Ahead of me was a row of cottages. I knocked on the door of the first one and asked for work of some sort, I was given a curt refusal. The second was no better, but the third yielded a pleasant request to go round to the back of the cottage where there was wood to be chopped. The old woman only wanted a few sticks and as there was already a pile cut for use I knew that she was simply doing this as an excuse to do me a kindness. She gave me a shilling. It was a fortune to me and there was more to follow — bread and cheese with a jug of cider in the woodshed. Rejuvenated, I thanked the woman in the way only a starving man can understand and set off to walk the three miles to the City of Manchester.

The waterways, on their snake-like courses, the hawthorn hedges, and the scattered cottages had given way to a rambling multitude of grey, dingy buildings and slum houses, which only served to depress my spirits even more. There is something uplifting about the country, but the opposite can be said of the town and city. But the country-bred lad had to learn the ways of the towns for, although he didn't realise it then, he was to spend a great part of his life in common lodging-houses which were to be found in every town along the length and breadth of the land.

3

BLOODY MARY'S

Although my belly was full and I was feeling happier for it, my feet were terribly blistered and each step was agony, but somehow I hobbled into the heart of the city. I needed a lodging-house but the one man certain to know their whereabouts was the one man I dare not ask — the policeman on his beat. Instead I asked a down-at-heel newsboy. He pointed with his thumb down an alley. I followed it to a vile looking building with a 'FULL UP' notice over the door. As I stared up at the tall house I shuddered for there was something nauseating about the place and a foul aroma of rancid food was belching out of the door which was wide open.

"We're full up, mate." The deputy of the house had come to the door and was standing with his thumbs twiddling with his braces, which were holding up a pair of grease-stained trousers. I almost said 'thank God for that' but stopped myself just in time. "Try Bloody Mary's down the lane, first left; they've got room. Tanner a night it is." his voice was kindly.

I thanked the man and went in search of Bloody Mary's. Much to my surprise the front door actually bore that name. I pushed it open and found myself in a hallway in which a tiny office was situated. A white-faced man was chewing tobacco at the same time cutting up a lump of the stuff into small pieces. He reeked of the stuff. "Want a kip, mate?" he asked.

I nodded and put my shilling down on the counter. He gave me sixpence change. "You're on the first landing, mate; take any bed what's vacant." He handed me a disc which bore the figure 1.

There were no questions asked, as in the spike, and immediately I felt an almost homely atmosphere, the place wasn't exactly a sweet-smelling bower but it was warm and I felt like a free human being and not an internee. I had no desire for food now and I felt conscious of my shaking hands as I glanced nervously, furtively around the huge kitchen. It was hardly likely that any of the Whiston spike men would be here, but I was extremely frightened just the same and wary of even looking men in the face. I still hadn't rid myself of the fear that at any second a hand would be placed on my shoulder. Gradually, however, I plucked up the courage to let my eyes take in the scene. There were at least forty men gathered together there. How many are police informers, I wondered? For lodging-houses were the hiding-holes of narks who seem to have the uncanny knack of spotting a guilty man in a crowd.

Public Health Acts came and went but the lodging-house owners did little to implement them and owning such a place was a nice steady source of income for very little outlay once the building was found and, as a rule, these decrepit places were a good investment. The owner was very rarely seen, usually being a remote figure, probably a prominent city man whose other activities would hardly be furthered if it was known that he owned a 'doss-house'. So he appointed a deputy as a 'front man' and paid him as little as possible, providing food and accommodation, and ignoring any ideas he had for making money on the side by selling tea or food. The house was kept just barely clean, as far as a brush and shovel will keep a place clean and, although token efforts were made from time to time to enforce rules for improving conditions by the Sanitary Inspectors, most of them slid back into old practices. Doss-houses were laws unto themselves and perhaps, only as good as the 'guests' deserved, but they were a necessity and the country was glad of them.

Imagine a large, several-storied terraced house; enter and, once having passed through the office hallway, come with me now into the main room of the house. The sleeping rooms are but secondary to the kitchen, for it is the kitchen which is the focal point of the lodging-house; the very heart of the place, and the prime piece in the kitchen is the fire. Everything revolves around it. To the man on the road the fire is paradise. He doesn't pay his tanner, or whatever, for the mangy, flea-ridden mattress; no, it is the fire he seeks when he enters a lodging-house for, winter or summer, it vomits out its coke fumes. Coke is the fuel of the doss-house and renders the atmosphere heavy, almost opium laden, if one wishes to strike a comparison with the seamen's dives' of foreign ports. Coke falls out in a greyish dust, but it warms a man and to the tramp heat is the Number One factor, whilst cold is his arch enemy.

So, we are in the kitchen which is gas-lit and full to overflowing with a motley collection of men, sitting, crouching and lying on an equally motley collection of benches, broken chairs and evil-smelling, but comfortable, settees. Humanity in all its sordid forms is here: tramps of the 'professional school', hard-liners of the road who know no other calling in life; there are others who have taken to the vagabond life out of sheer necessity and lack of regular work; the street beggar is here with his shifty, ever watchful eyes probing into the pockets and hearts of the other men, and is usually a permanent resident of the place; here, too, are the casual workmen, the navvies who have drunk the money they have made and can afford nowhere better to stay; the paper 'boys' (most of this breed are over sixty); drifters, loafers, men coming, men going, sometimes on the road to somewhere but more often on the road to nowhere; men who want work and can't find it, often young lads such as I was then, and men who won't work and live off those who do — a cross section of life's unlovely folk. There is the odd woman dotted about, for some houses allow this and provide special rooms for them to sleep in and, if the deputy is corrupt and the women are agreeable, a customer can always be found for them for a trade it does not need me to describe. For a woman need never starve on the road. Add, for good measure, the physically handicapped; the babbling drunk who is perpetually shaking, pick-pockets and the men on the run from the law, the queers and the ponces, then the brew is complete; a human broth composed of society's cast-offs and dregs, decent or otherwise, they are the scrapings of life's vast barrel.

Every man Jack of them is engaged in some form of

pastime just the same as in every kitchen or parlour of every house in the land, for *this* is home to the homeless man. Two fellows are playing Three-card Brag on a form, another group are playing dominoes for pinches of tea or snuff, there are two bruiser-looking navvies arm wrestling and cussing as they do it, another is cutting his corns with a razor-blade next to a chap eating chips out of a newspaper. The man 'not right in the head' is babbling to himself in imbecilic fashion, while on his left is a doss-house politician speaking on behalf of the Reforming Committee who are trying to form a union for the protection of the rights of men on the road, and ten years on you meet the same man and not one step further has he got in his efforts to form a 'united front'; on his left sits a man with a long white beard who looks like Jesus of Nazareth and sings hymns which he alternates with snatches of psalms.

And in the centre of all this chatter and hubbub, smoke and gloom, is the fire. It is enclosed in a stove which has a flat top with room for pots and pans or other utensils, such as cocoa tins, metal lids and other makeshift containers. The pots and pans are bubbling and spitting all day long in the kitchen as men prepare their meals, but evening is the main time for the great fry-up of scraps 'borrowed', begged or stolen or, in some cases, genuinely purchased. Any tramp worth his salt will always produce something for the evening fry-up, be it a piece of bacon, eggs, or a chop if he's lucky.

There is the classic tramp tale of the old veteran who went out of the doss-house one Sunday dinner-time and knocked on the door of a house and asked the woman if she could borrow her Sunday joint to make himself some gravy!

And what a smell rises up as fowl, fish, and pig sizzle and fry in the same communal pan. Lodging-house frying-pans are more like dust-bin lids. Each man watches his own tasty bit with the devotion of a sentinel, take your eye off it for a second and hey-presto! It has gone. The speed of the hand deceives the eye. Your piece of succulent bacon has vanished, but when your eyes pierce the gloom they see small pieces of bacon, vaguely familiar, sizzling in another pan. Caution and a close watch is the order of the day and it is a wonder murders aren't committed daily over the business of cooking supper at the lodging-house stove. And tramps are nothing if not economical for in a huge saucepan are a couple of turnips stolen from a field, or potatoes in their jackets, but they are not the sole occupants of the pan for boiling alongside them is a pair of socks perhaps or a shirt having its annual boil. Over the stove are the drying racks, suspended from the ceiling, which hold clothes in varying stages of drying so that if a man sits below them he has to keep moving his head to avoid the drips.

But of all the pastimes and chores in the kitchen tea-making and drinking is the most popular. The tramp is a champion tea-drinker and there is a well-known saying on the road that the average tramp consumes enough tea in a year to sink Tommy Lipton's yacht. Whether it is in the lodging-house or by the side of the road, the tramp will be seen to be making tea – 'drumming up' as it is called amongst the tramps. The religion of the road. And just as I had discovered in Liverpool, tea is a common form of barter.

Kindness is present, too. Let that be stated firmly. A man with no food will not starve. Someone will give him food and no man will go to bed without a mug of tea to warm his belly. But if a man is found to be a cadger then his tap is immediately stopped. There is a degree of kindness on the road for a man genuinely reduced to starvation level.

* * * *

Unless you have given the deputy a back-hander, you are not allowed to sleep in the kitchen at night and the trouble is that, by the time the call to go above is given, often you have had a sleep in the warm, heavy atmosphere conducive to slumber so that when you manage to rouse yourself and leave the kitchen behind you are met by a cold dampness which chills the limbs, and the higher you go in the house the colder it becomes. There is no heat in the sleeping quarters and the only light is from a single gas mantle. An iron door greets me on Number One landing. This is the communal bedroom. There is a dank, mildewy smell of rotting vegetation or is it rotting humanity? The room is tightly crammed with beds, side by side. Iron-framed contraptions bearing lousy mattresses and a couple of blankets that look as if they were laundered in a coalmine. In some houses there are no beds, only mattresses, so that you lie head to head, breathing into one another's faces. And, common to doss-house and spike, the single latrine stands underneath the window which is boarded up with planks and old sacks. If sleep does come in such a place it can only be in fits and starts, for the coughing and wheezing is dreadful to listen to, a disgusting symphony of farm-yard noises. One man is having a nightmare, sobbing for a while, then suddenly screaming. Another is yelling at him and threatening to break his so-and-so neck. Another is shouting for his mother. I lie there, shivering and listening to every sound, but happy in the knowledge that no one can steal my boots without me knowing, unless they do so forcibly. Though I am a novice, I know from Clive the golden rule in the doss-house kip room — always sleep with your clothes under your pillow, if there is one; if not, then use them as a pillow, for unlike spikes the bedroom of the lodging-house isn't locked and men come and go as they please. "They'd separate you from yer breath, mate, if they could" is certainly a truism.

*   *   *   *

As I lay there I relived the events of the day. It seemed impossible that it had all taken place in the space of a single day. I thought of old Teddy Bear and said a silent prayer to God that the tramp-major was not dead. My chances of getting any of the witnesses to speak up on my behalf were very slight. Such men were wary of the police and would be very loath to cooperate. For I had attacked a casual ward official. A mere tramp-major maybe but, compared to my place in society, like comparing a prince to a pauper. The punishment of the law was very severe for such offences, for it protected its purveyors and I knew I had little chance if I was caught — and if he was dead, well I knew only too well the punishment for that. It seemed to me cruel justice that a rat of a man like Fred should have the umbrella of authority to hide under. I, too, fell to cursing the System and the Government which implemented it. I cursed the twist of fate that had sent me on a round of squalor and shame. After all, I simply desired to work. I didn't realise it then, but the resentment of the chronic tramp was building up inside me and I was growing into a bitter man.

The man in the next 'bed' refused to stop talking, despite threats to strangle him if he didn't 'belt up'. He was violently condemning politicians and Lloyd George in particular. The poor chap came in for a worse slating than the Kaiser; "You knew where yer stood with Kaiser Bill, but this old sod's nowt but a butter mouthed typical politician. Promise yer the bloody earth and then give yer sod all. Country fit for bleedin' heroes, 'e promised, and where am I now? Sleepin' in a bloody flea palace, that's where, and where's 'e bloody well kippin', I'd like to know? Why in some swank 'otel, more an' likely. Aye an' with a full belly an' all, yer can bank on that! The bloody arystockery's the trouble behind the mess we're in, all wind and bullshit they are. You scratch my shaggin' back and I'll scratch yours. Democracy? I thought we won the blinkin' war? They use you, mate, that's what they do, blinkin' use you and then throw you on the scrap heap. One law for the bleedin' rich and one for the bleedin' poor, always was and always will be." It was the same old story I was to hear so often from old soldiers embittered with their lot in life, but the truth of the matter with a lot of old sweats is that they become so institutionalised by the army, for the Service is the biggest institution of them all, making men feel lost when they leave it so they seek another institution to protect them, such as prison. I met many regular old soldiers, N.C.O's and Officers amongst them, who found life outside the army impossible. Often they had been little tin gods in a close-knit community, but in the outside world they were nobody's. And that can be cruelly hard to take.

The voice prattled on and on in a litany of moaning and grumbling. At last I drifted away into a state of semi-consciousness. I remember a voice saying "Belt up, this ain't Hyde bleedin' Corner, mate!" and then I must have passed into a deep sleep.

I don't know how long I slept, but I was suddenly awakened by the clanging of metal and a dreadful oath. Someone had knocked over the latrine bucket.

"Why the! — "

"What the! — "

A flash of light illuminated the room for a few seconds. There was an angry roar followed by a flood of invectives. Then:

"Out of it, you lot! Out of it, I say — come on, look sharp!"

Another flash of light, brighter, more powerful this time, and I saw a plump white face behind a lamp.

"It's the bloody polis!" screeched an Irish voice.

"Jaysus, yous is right, Michael!" seconded another.

The man who hated Lloyd George's guts was snoring like a pig, oblivious to it all.

"I said out of it!" roared the copper.

"Line 'em up, constable, won't yer . . . for god's sake, line 'em up!" This was a fresh voice. A burly uniformed man was in the room now and I could see the stripes of a sergeant on his sleeves.

"Come on — come on — come on — out — out of it! Every man Jack of you — out!"

"The polis — polis — Jaysus, it's the polis!"

"Out you get, Paddy." The constable started prodding and probing with his truncheon and Michael, the Irishman, obliged instantly, invoking the help of all the saints he could think of. After a lot of shouting from the policemen and objections from the inmates, we were herded down the stairs and into the kitchen. If I hadn't been so terrified, for I knew my freedom was at an end, I would have rejoiced, for the heat of the room met us in an enveloping blanket of instant comfort.

"Line up, you lot!" bawled the sergeant. "And light the ruddy gas, will you. Talk about the black 'ole of Calcutta."

"I'll do it, Sergeant." I recognised the voice of the deputy eager to please.

"You'd not recognise your own mother in this bloody light," said one of the constables as the thin, reedy light turned the murky, grey figures into forms recognisable as men. Despite the heat, I was quivering now. I felt sick and I knew it was simply a matter of time — seconds, at the most minutes.

It took a little time to round up the stragglers and line us up into some semblance of order. At last the parade of grotesque and tragi-comical inmates, in varying stages of dress and undress, was ready and a hush descended which was broken only by the hissing sound of a man making water in the fire. A young constable shouted to the man to stop it.

"Let him finish," said the sergeant. "This ain't the Midland Hotel, me lad. You're going to be educated tonight, lad." The young constable, hardly older than myself, shuffled his feet uncomfortably and some of the men laughed.

"Now then, as this is England it's my duty to tell you why I've got you up from your comfortable beds at this hour." The sergeant was moving along the line which almost encircled the kitchen by this time as the last risers from the top floors were slotted into position in the human ring. "It's an identity parade, see. Right, Constable, tell the deputy to show Mr Braintree in will you."

As I was the youngest man in the circle the identification was a mere formality as far as I was concerned. "You're shaking, mate," a voice whispered in my ear and I shook all the more for the reminder.

A tall, well-dressed man was led in by a constable. Police reinforcements had arrived and two constables stood by the door with truncheons raised. I peered hard at the man, I had never seen him before but couldn't help but compare the smartness of his attire with the room and its unkempt occupants.

"Now take your time, sir," said the sergeant. "Walk right round and if you see the man place your right hand on his shoulder."

"I understand, officer," answered the man in a refined voice. "But my mind is already made up. There is your man." The sergeant gave a whistle of surprise. The witness's tall figure was in front of me, his eyes gimlets of fire in a pale face. He took two steps on the tiled floor, booming steps — strident, piercingly sharp in my eardrums. The sounds and the man fused into a whirlpool of pounding, visual terror in my brain. "Are you sure, sir?" The voice of the law reverberated in my head, its volume multiplied by the fear-stricken panic inside me.

"Positive, officer. There is no doubt." The ginger-headed fellow who had been eating chips from the paper earlier on stepped forward and the handcuffs were snapped into position on his wrists. Death could not have been whiter than that face of his. I tried to speak but couldn't. I fought for spittle to moisten my lips. With an effort, I asked the man next to me what he had done.

"Raped a woman in Eccles last night. You'd have thought he'd 'ave scarpered further than Manchester, wouldn't yer?"

My legs buckled from under me and I collapsed in a heap on the floor.

4

GRIM TIMES

I awoke exactly in the same spot where I had fallen, only some kind soul had placed a cushion underneath my head. A cushion in a doss-house! I never had the luxury of one afterwards. Like finding a water-bucket in Hell. The dead stench of the room savaged my nostrils as I tried to focus my heavy-lidded eyes on objects, strange objects, for I had been dreaming. And in the way of dreams, once awake, I had already forgotten the subject of my dreaming, but I am sure it was of home. And so, for quite half a minute I didn't fully realise where I was. Then I recalled the ordeal of the identity parade and felt a wave of relief engulf me; then my nostrils picked up another smell — of fried bacon! Some lucky devil had left-overs for breakfast. This man at the stove was fat, an unusual sight in such surroundings, for corpulence and lodging-houses were a rare marriage. I vaguely recognised him as an occupant of one of the beds. As he turned from the stove, with the bacon still in the pan, two men rose to their feet. One pinioned the fat man's arms while the other kneed him viciously in the groin. The bacon-fryer uttered an agonising groan then slumped in a heap on the floor. The pan was placed on a table and the bacon shared out beween them as unconcernedly as if it were a daily happening.

"I'd swing for the swine only I've more respect for me neck," said the man who had done the deed.

"Leave 'im be now," said his mate. "What Ginger done he deserves to be topped for, but I don't 'old with informers, no matter what a man's done."

And that was the end of the matter as far as the rest of

them were concerned, as they passed to and fro over the recumbent body, not caring whether they stood on him or not. Lodging-house justice was like that, enacted quickly and without fuss.

I couldn't help but think to myself how this doldrum society slouched out into the street to greet the new day. One would have thought they were men going to their death by hanging, they looked so loath to leave the warm kitchen. By chance, I happened to be walking alongside a grey-whiskery old chap whose boots could have tramped the highways of the world or across a thousand deserts. He looked almost incapable of anything resembling speed but, in a flash, he had left my side and was fingering a silver coin he had picked up in the gutter. "A tosheroon!" he cried, and flung the coin into the air and caught it again. This he repeated with relish. "A whole tosheroon! Lady Fortune has smiled on me to-day." He was talking to himself, but suddenly caught sight of the envy in my eyes. What else he read in them I don't know, but they excited pity in the old man. "You were with me, mate. We'll go halves. Are you hungry?"

"I feel as if I'm starving to death," I answered.

"Aye and I wouldn't doubt that. A half-a-crown means breakfast for two. We'll dine like dukes you and me, come on."

"You are very kind," I said.

"Look, mate, if it was one of the other bastards I wouldn't give 'em a crust of bread, but you look a youngster to me. I mean, well, you don't look like the rest of 'em in there. Down on your luck?"

"You could say that. I'm looking for a job."

"And good luck to yer, mate! But come to think of it, I might be able to help." He was speaking as he led me, as fast as his wobbling legs could carry him, into Market Street. And what a smell was in that street. Simply the smell of frying bacon from one small coffee shop but to me the whole street was flooded by a savoury aroma that blotted out all other senses, all other thoughts, lustful to my taste buds that had not yet tasted. And when I did eat it was with a wild-beast greed over which I had no control. I have experienced hunger many times since then, but never a hunger so intense. I have since read in library books that shock can cause hunger, for mine was not the usual feeling of emptiness with which I am familiar. The night's ordeal had told its tale.

The old man had told the girl to give us breakfast for two to the value of half-a-crown. I remember that she took the coin off him first. The bacon and eggs were followed with lashings of toast, coffee and hot rolls.

"Feel better, lad?" he asked and I could not answer him. "I heard of a job going down Swinton way. It's a good pad out of town, mind, but you'll feel a new man now. It's a garage name of Miller's. Heard as they were wanting someone only yesterday. Ask for the name when you get there and anyone will tell yer where it is. Now I'm off on the mooch, regular beat I has, but you get a job if you can, mate."

"I'm very grateful," I said.

"I know you are," said the old fellow, patting my shoulder. Then he was gone. One of the many countless trampships who pass in the night.

In the light of what followed, I believe now that breakfast saved my life for it was two whole days before I ate again accept for a crust of bread I salvaged from a bin. Miller's garage had taken a man on that very morning. What followed is now almost lost in a haze and only fragments of what I endured in those fruitless months of job-seeking remain. And so, I am unable to put down in any order or sequence the events of that period or even recall for how long it lasted. I do recall sleeping under a bridge, then nights spent in doorways; I still hear the voice of the law telling me to move on, 'Can't doss here, mate', and I also recall receiving enough money for a night's lodging and half a loaf of bread and two ounces of dripping. What small job I did in return time has erased from my memory. There were times when I was given work, sufficient simply to earn enough for my kip. Somehow I kept going, desperately striving to keep alive, let alone work. Sometimes I was given coppers and food, but I can honestly state that I have never openly begged on the streets. I peddled with a 'bible' (card of laces, buttons, elastic, etc.) and later on I learned how to trick people out of money, but I was never an outright beggar. More honest to beg than rob, you might say, but pride is a man's worst enemy. But, new to the road, I was then still an upright, virtuous young man with no other desire but to obtain steady work, which is the right of every man. But to feed an empty, aching belly supersedes all other desires. Nothing can eradicate the vivid recollections I have of some of the habitations I was forced to use for a night's shelter.

How often people who are tired say that they could sleep on a clothes line. It is so easy to say, it falls off the tongue so glibly. How many know the origin of the expression and how many have actually done it? It may have been in Bolton or perhaps it was Bury, it matters little. All I know is that I had twopence in the whole world to rattle on a tombstone. I asked at a lodging-house if they had any cheap accommodation. "Twopenny kip at the back, mate. Better grab a space pronto," said the deputy. The 'twopenny kip' was a long narrow room full of slouching humanity. For a few seconds my mind could not absorb the scene or form any conclusion as to what these men might be doing. I had reached the doldrums of trampdom; then I was aware that the men were slouching across a rope which stretched from one end of the room to the other, fastened to the wall at each end by hook and staple. Mercifully it was situated directly behind the kitchen wall housing the communal stove which made the rope-room warm. I followed suit and leaned on the rope with them. Weariness did the rest and, strange though it may seem to those who only know the comfort of a clean snug bed, I slept better than I had done in many a doss-house. But what a rude awakening was in store for me! Think of it: twenty or so contorted bodies slumped across a rope; snoring, wheezing, coughing, striving for position in order to sleep the better. The hour of seven o'clock strikes, a whistle is blown and half a minute is given to straighten up and quit the rope. But how many men are awake? And how many *can* straighten up after a night spent bending like broken slaves asleep at the oars? Few. Too bad, then, for no more warning is given; one end of the rope is released and down go the men, like the ten green bottles of the nursery rhyme. Such, then, is the rope-room and even as late as 1937 I heard that such places still existed in London. And yet children at school to-day read Dickens and wonder if such things really happened in his days. They happened in the twentieth century also.

In Preston I used the mission or the 'sit-up', as it was known to men who frequented it. It was the same price as the rope-room but by no means as comfortable. 'Proud Preston' is one of my favourite towns and I stayed there often for it possessed some of the best lodging-houses on the road. But the sit-up was one establishment it had no right to be proud of, shelter to the homeless man it did provide but it went no further than that. I used it one icy cold night, the staccato sounds I heard were the chattering of teeth and the shuddering of numbed frozen bodies. The only furniture in the room were kneelers made of hard wood, similar to the type used in churches but without the necessary padding for more comfortable praying. But instead of knees resting on them they were pillows for heads, so that the occupants lay on the stone floor, as one would lie in bed, with their head on the hard wood. The mission was christened the 'sit-up' by the attitude adopted by the fortunate ones who had a kneeler next to the wall. They could sit on it as a variation to the prone position, their backs against the wall.

Strange, but in all my wanderings, only on a very rare occasion did I use a shelter run by a religious group. I find my attitude of mind difficult to explain. To receive a rebuff from a clergyman then, further along the street, to be given the price of your night's kip by a prostitute makes a man wonder where goodness begins and evil ends, and vice versa. Life, so black and white when it is taught to a child by its parents and Sunday school teacher, takes on quite different hues when sampled and judged as a whole. The blacks are often not quite so black and the whites are a murky grey. In another town, a few days after the clergyman had urged me to 'get out of it and get yourself a job', I was invited into a Manse kitchen and given a meal by the wife of another clergyman. I felt as if Almighty God Himself had stepped in to tilt the scales His way and restore a little balance to the perplexed mind of a young man who had firmly believed that all men acted as did their counterparts in the Bible.

I don't doubt that the people who ran these religious charities were well intentioned, they simply translated the

Bible wrongly. Take the 'prayer and a bun' hut in Liverpool, they made you pray and sing first then gave you the tea and bun afterwards. If that isn't bribery what is?

If I know my Christ then I am sure He would have given us the bun first then asked us afterwards if we wanted to pray with Him. Christ does not force, does not bribe, He gives every man his choice. Consequently, I have met men who would sooner starve than enter a religious shelter and there was one incident in Blackburn which I shall never forget.

In was Sunday evening, church bells were ringing, and I was trying to keep warm in a shop doorway. Across the street was a small chapel and I could hear the hymn singing. I even joined in one of them for I had been a member of the Church Choir in my Cheshire village. My ability to sing was to stand me in good stead later on. Coming along the street in the direction of the chapel was someone who appeared to be half beast and half man, a wild savagery about him that I had never seen in any other man and, as he came nearer, I saw bloodshot madness in his eyes. Lank hair hung down his back in dirty rivulets and his face was covered with a beard, only his eyes giving the certainty that here was actually a human being. I can so describe him because I had seen him earlier in the day begging. He was mad with hunger and ravaged every bin he came to on his slow progression down the long street; by the time he came close to the church the congregation were emerging. Most of them steered clear of him and shepherded their offsprings from his path, some stared at him in contempt, but one white-faced young lad approached him with a basket. He had waited until most of the people had departed and then he handed the man the basket without anyone else seeing. "Here, there's food in this — take it, please."

"Piss off . . . you bloody Bible thumper . . .." The man cursed bitterly, madly, and would have struck the youth if he hadn't turned away quickly. The bin scrounger continued on his task, slowly moving along the street. The youth stood still for a moment, in order to gather his thoughts it seemed. Then, as if suddenly inspired, he dashed down the street where there were three gas lamps in a row, each one with a waste-bin attached. I saw him put something in the first bin, then into the second, then the third. And then he left, glancing behind him as he ran hoping that the tramp had not seen him. I will never forget the shout that half savage creature gave as his hands salvaged a loaf of bread from the bin. He tore it apart like a prairie dog tears at its captured prey. In turn, he visited the two other bins and in each, to his utter amazement, there was food! What a feast this street pariah had, little knowing that it had been provided by the young chap he had so cruelly spurned. I have read texts on charity and listened to sermons given from open-air pulpits, but no text, no sermon explained to me the true meaning of charity so clearly as did the action of that young man in Blackburn. He did not want to impress others, or impress God, he simply saw a starving man and wanted to help him and found a means of doing so. I could even picture the Good God laughing to Himself at the young fellow's ingenuity!

*   *   *   *

Although I wasn't immediately made aware of it, England was at the end of its two year post-war boom in industry. Following the war, the hopes for a thriving country were fulfilled in a harvest of industrial output which brought a period of hectic prosperity, prompted by the public's desire to spend in order to compensate for the lean years of austerity and war-imposed rationing. I had not been able to get employment during the tail-end of this period of plenty so my chances of obtaining work now grew worse as the tempo of the times altered dramatically as the country was hit by strikes. Wholesale sackings were now the order of the day as the strikers refused to return to work. The short halcyon days were over and disenchanted, disillusioned men were given the alternative of returning to work for less wages or joining the ever-growing army of unemployed. The signs of the times were mirrored by the sights in every town I passed through. Gangs of men on every mean street corner; soap-box orators roaring and ranting; silent smokeless factories and shuttered warehouses. "Russia has the right answer," one fellow boomed continually on a street corner in Wigan. "The Comm-unist Party is the answer." I can recall how he hyphonated the word.

Although the immediate post-war boom had made England an industrially prosperous country for a short while, the men who had fought for her wanted more money; they wanted improved conditions and an increase in wages. They wanted and expected a reward for their service to their country. They got nothing. From being a country with no unemployment problem (the history books tell us this but, of course, there were unemployed, men too, though in the light of past and future standards they were a small percentage) we became a country of discontented men who felt cheated and robbed; the post-war spending spree was over, prices dropped and so did wages. A kick in the teeth for the heroes so blithely spoken about in Parliament. The effects of the strikes and the depression in trade were apparent everywhere.

By the end of 1921 over 2,000,000 men were unemployed. The mean streets became meaner; the people I passed were becoming crestfallen wrecks; the women-folk striving vainly to keep themselves and their families respectable. It was a period of dole queues, soup-kitchens, over-crowded workhouses, an increase in prostitution, prosperity for pawnbrokers, and an overall feeling of doom that the situation was not going to improve. Of course, what came later was worse, far worse — the General Strike, hunger marches and depressions, and yet I was apart from it all. I was not married and therefore had no grasping kids to feed. I was alone, only myself to look after. If I went under then no one would miss me. I would be branded neither a success nor a failure, for I was a nonentity. I was an island. Every tramp is an island.

And so, as I roamed through those depressed towns of a once-thriving Lancashire, I began to realise that one man with no ties can exist. I even began to feel lucky. A tramp was in the making. I would become a 'real' tramp, work was out of the question now, so I would accept that I was a tramp but, in doing so, it would not be a degraded, deprived acceptance of a beggar's life. No, I would work at the trade. I would learn and I would apply to the trade of being a tramp the same energy and seriousness any other young apprentice would apply to his chosen profession. For once a man accepts his position he can then advance and better himself with the means at his disposal. I was young and healthy, despite my recent life, and I had only myself to fend for. If I failed or died of starvation then I was a fool. And I was entering trampdom at a time when thousands of other men were taking to the roads; it was not going to be easy but, in comparison to those bleak, black, seemingly endless months of job seeking, I felt a lightness of heart — a relief almost — for I knew that my life ahead could certainly not be any worse.

It was quite astonishing how many clerkish types were on the road, some through the most amazing quirks of fate. Often it was much harder for a clerical worker to find employment than a manual worker. In Warrington I met a young chap with a very similar background to my own. He had had a very unhappy home life but had found a most interesting job as a costing clerk with a firm in Leeds and had lived in 'digs'. Disaster struck when his firm went bankrupt so he sought after work in the city but to no avail until, unable to pay his weekly rent, he took to the road seeking work. Like me, he found that returning Servicemen were filling the posts and soon, through living rough, his appearance deteriorated rapidly. He was forced to pawn all but the clothes he wore. I met him only five weeks after he had left Leeds but already his chances of employment were gone. He had done no wrong; his 'crime' was that he was dishevelled, poorly shod and living like a pauper. He was on the slippery slope, in the state of downward progression I, too, was in. He had applied for a job only to be met with the same reception I experienced in Liverpool, "Do you have to look so dirty though?" he was asked. What sort of sanctimonious idiot would ask such a question? How could you keep clean when you were forced to live in doss-houses? It was impossible to be any other way. Let a man once be down and it was almost an impossibility to get up again. What little money this lad made he fed himself with, there was none left for soap or new clothes. He was pitched into a communal bedroom with thieves and beggars, an honest lad out to find a job, a young lad of some sensitivity it was obvious, he spoke the king's English perfectly, was well mannered and gentle. The fact that he had received a good education was at once apparent, but to what end? Where else to go than the common lodging-house? They didn't have class divisions there. Once you had paid your money you were one of the lodgers — on a level with the street moocher, the jailbird and the thief, not mattering one jot how a man spoke or at which school he was educated when he was in the abyss of the doss-house. "I have despaired of ever getting a job," he told me. Yet he had been trying for only five weeks. The life was abhorrent to him, he was ashamed of his position. Life had not provided him with the armaments to fight such a battle and yet he was full of courage, not realising that I had been trying to obtain similar work for over nine months, so what chance had he? Still I didn't disillusion him, take away a man's hope and he is finished. Like me, he was hearing a recital of petty crimes nightly in the doss-house, surrounded by professional scroungers. They lived far better than he did and yet they had no desire to work. These were the sort the genuine out-of-work man had to associate with. They laughed at the lad looking for work, branded him a 'young mug'.

Our structure of learning provides us with schools and universities. Lower down the scale we had doss-houses and prisons. The doss-house was the school, prison was the university and when qualification day dawned out came the scholars to go back to the 'schools', but this time as teachers, nay professors, passing on the lessons they had learned. I doubt whether a saint could have lived in a doss-house for long without losing his insignia of sainthood. His halo would have been slightly askew, for sure.

"It makes you wonder why folk bother to earn a decent living when you listen to these fellows," said my companion. "Some of them sound as if they enjoy the life." Already, like myself, he was contaminated by their philosophy. Take away a man's livelihood and the devil has him by the forelock.

"I would like to get hold of that man who asked you why

you were dirty and forcibly bring him here," I told him, angrily. "Then I would strip him of all his money except enough for a kip. Then I'd leave him alone on the streets and let him see if *he* could keep clean, and if he could find another job when his shoe-leather was full of holes and his office suit tattered and dirty." He began to argue against me, making out that no office manager could dream of employing a down-and-out. He said:

"Of course, if you were to say that to such a man he would scoff and say 'but it couldn't happen to me'. No, I never dreamed for one second that it could have happened to me either. Once I thought of myself as a respectable clerk. I was smug, I suppose. You know, I remember telling a poor fellow not to scrounge and go off and find a job of work. And I had a pocketful of coins. How can people realise fully what it is like on the seamier side until they have tried it for themselves?"

*   *   *   *

This lad had never been strong, now he was terribly thin and pale and told me over a mug of tea how he had spent months on end in sanatoriums when a young boy. Already, after those few weeks, he was no longer fit to work. Compared to his five weeks on the streets, I was a veteran and tempted to tell him about the workhouses, but felt that he was humiliated enough. He looked consumptive to my eyes, yet a photograph taken at his office Christmas party showed a good-looking thin young man, not in the full vigour of healthy manhood even then but, my God, what a difference nice clothes and decent meals can make to a man. Those five weeks he had endured were longer to him than five years would have been to me. How right my observations were for only a month later I met him on a street corner in Ashton-under-Lyne — he was singing for coppers, and he was dying, there was no mistaking the signs. He passed away less than a week later in a lodging-house in Manchester. Ha'pence worth of bread and scraps of scrag-end were not the sole cause of his death. He had died of shame, for I had met him and he had opened his heart and soul to me in circumstances where a man is only capable of telling the truth.

The tragedy of Philip's sudden fall to the dust-level of society and his subsequent death was the kick I needed to shake myself free from my own futile seeking after work. They could keep it and stuff it up their sanctimonious backsides. If someone had approached me then and asked me to describe on paper my occupation I would have written *tramp*.

I had made up my mind — or had it been made up for me? I will let the social historians answer that one.

A tramp was born.

5

THE ROAD BECKONS

It was in Preston that I had reached my decision to make tramping my livelihood and it was as good a place as any to begin. And, having made this decision, my luck changed for the better. I met a chap in the lodging-house who promised to introduce me to a contact on the next morning. As it was Market Day, he said there would be casual work going if I wanted it. So the next day I followed the fellow like an extra shadow in case he should go off without me or offer the job to someone else.

We arrived early in the Market Square and, already, the stall-holders were setting out their merchandise. Large bare-armed women in striped aprons were unloading boxes of eggs and poultry they had brought in from the country. Most of them had been up all night preparing for Market Day. Some were plucking fowls and feathers and innards were scattered over the cobbles.

As trade got under way I recognised several of the men with whom I had shared the kip-room at the doss-house. One was selling *Old Moore's Almanacs;* another peddling cough candy whilst another walked up and down the street carrying a Sandwich-board. Preston Market Day represented a decent day's takings to these tramps. As I stood with my new found companion I began to wonder who the contact would be. Just then there was a sharp whistle which was immediately recognisable to my mate because straight away he led me through the maze of passages around the stalls. On a corner of the Market Place we were greeted by a flashily-dressed character whose label could have been 'cheap and shoddy' for he was the epitome of the street shark – the fast-talking salesman who could sell water to Neptune and sand to the Israelites. "Ears still sharp I see, Wilf," he greeted my pal.

"I could tell your whistle anywhere, Mr Smith," said Wilf. "This 'ere's Joe."

Mr Smith slapped me heartily on the shoulder. "Do a good job, Joe, and you'll get paid fair and proper. Here, for gawds's sake, put this mac over your jacket. You look as if you ain't got twopence in the world."

"I haven't," I answered, with a grin.

"But you will have, my son – work well for honest Jim Smith the Bargain King and you'll eat well tonight, my son." He breathed garlic into my nostrils.

Wilf then gave me my instructions. We were to be employed as 'kidders'. 'Kidding' is an old tramp trade and a good day's work if it can be obtained. Every Market 'Bargain' salesman and pavement merchant has his 'kidder'. 'Honest' Jim Smith was selling hosiery. This was only one of the various lines in which he specialised, buying a line in bulk then spending two or three days on the one item until it was sold out. After that it would be something else, perhaps slippers or gloves. Our job was to stimulate trade. The secret of the game is to stand well apart and enthuse over the goods offered for sale. We were the bellows to fan the onlookers into purchasers.

"It works this way, Joe," said Wilf, who had worked for 'Honest Jim' on many occasions. "Jim will start off shouting the price for a pair of stockings – say four shillings. Well, I'll put me hand in the air and shout up but Jim won't take the sale. He'll shout up 'Hold on, friend. I know they're a bargain at four shillings but they don't call me 'Honest Jim' for nothing' and all the rest of the gabble. So he'll drop 'em to three and sixpence then you'll shout up all eager to buy, but he'll give you the old tale again, he don't want to 'do' anybody, not 'Honest Jim' what's been coming to Preston for years – and so on – see? Get 'em going, you see, make 'em think as you and me know a good thing when we sees one. Eventually, when the stockings is down to one and six, I'll shout up, thrusting the money at him. Jim takes it. Then you push forward and so it starts – we've got 'em going.

Then when we've done that we go off across to his wife's place and do the same. She sells saucepans. Then it's back to Jim's again and so on for each time there's a fresh crowd. Got it? Come on then, mate."

Wilf couldn't have painted a more accurate picture for it worked exactly as he had described. After collecting the money for the first sale from Jim's assistant we made our purchases then handed the parcels back to him in a concealed place behind another stall. The hosiery went back into stock and then we were given money to go to the saucepan stall — and on it went until three o'clock in the afternoon.

Business on both stalls was very brisk. Jim's stocking patter was very clever but it was a wonder that some of his ribald remarks about the female anatomy didn't earn him a black eye. I must have purchased a half gross each of stockings and saucepans. Jim and his wife were making a small fortune selling inferior articles at an exaggerated price. A good 'kidder' is worth his weight in gold to a Market salesman. For our six hours work we got two shillings apiece, with an offer to meet him in Clitheroe on the next day. Not exactly gold but a good wage to me.

Wilf then wanted me to go and tour the pubs 'griddling'. This is the tramp word for hymn singing in the street. I knew enough about it to be aware that it was a trade in which a man with a pathetic sobbing voice comes off best. My training as a choral singer in the church choir and an inbred love of music made me rebellious to such a suggestion. Wilf went off on his own, saying I was a silly bugger, for two could do better than one at 'griddling'. I saw him later on, standing outside a tavern, singing 'Rock of Ages'. A coyote baying at the moon was a prize-winning vocalist compared to Wilf's adenoidal screeching of the well-loved hymn. But the true 'griddler' is no mug. He knows that hymns, especially performed on the Sabbath, are good catch-pennies. It is difficult for some people, nay impossible, to pass a chap with a down-on-his-heels-rips-in-his-backside look about him without a pang of conscience. "Singing hymns, the poor man. Shows he's a true Christian despite it all," I heard a woman remark as she put a silver coin in Wilf's hat. The same

Wilf was one of the biggest blackguards on the road and spent a five-year stretch in Strangeways many years later. But for wringing the withers of a church-going old lady he had no equal. And for 'screwing' church offertory boxes he had no equal either.

It was on that day I saw a famous Preston character, known as Flycatcher Joe. He was an itinerant pedlar who wandered the streets selling his home-made fly-papers at two for a penny. The substance he spread on the paper was called 'tuttle'. He always wore a tall hat wrapped round with the papers, which were covered with flies and blue-bottles. His cry of, 'Catch 'em alive! Blue-bottles and flies — catch 'em alive!' was famous in Preston and surrounding villages. One butcher always gave him twopence to stand well away from his shop because he claimed that the sight of Joe's fly-infested headpiece was enough to sour the stomach of his customers and put them off meat. Joe would never leave until he got his twopence.

I heard of Joe's death, a few weeks later, on the tramp grapevine.

With the money I had earned I set out to buy a stock for peddling. Most back-street draper shops sold quantities of buttons on cards and elastic to street pedlars at wholesale prices. I invested eighteen pence on a small stock and kept the sixpence for my doss. For the rest of the day I stood in the gutter, pushing my buttons and elastic cards into the faces of passers-by. I collected a shilling in coppers. But no tramp wants to sell his wares if he can avoid it. They are merely bait for sympathy money. Some folk will simply give the exact price asked; others will say 'keep the change' and others will give the tramp a few coppers and then refuse the proffered goods. The type the tramp detests is the person who thinks he is doing him a great favour by purchasing the whole card. Thus, the tramp's stock-in-trade has been taken away from him. A card of buttons worth retail, say, two shillings can bring a lucky pedlar three or even four shillings and sometimes more.

Right on that very first day I began to learn the artifices of tramp lore. So, with my stock in my sack, I started to give some thought to my future route. Wilf had impressed upon me the necessity of keeping to one circuit. A man who calls regularly builds up confidence in those who give him tea and food, and a place to sleep. This is one of the most important facts of the road. The Public Library was still open so I was able to ponder over a map of the country north of Preston. The towns and villages were but names to me. Wilf had told me that there was nice country to the north but I had no idea then that the North of England possessed a softer side. At school I had learned about the cotton-mills and the coalmining and I had had first-hand experience of the grime and squalor of these Industrial places. I made a resolution in that library to serve my apprenticeship in the country districts during the Spring and Summer and move back into the towns for the Winter. For the most parts, my tramping life hardly varied this routine.

Next day I told Wilf I wouldn't be going with him to Clitheroe to work for Honest Jim. He said I was a fool to try to make my living by going North but I determined to try. A few miles tramp out of Preston, on the Lancaster road, I got a lift in a farmer's cart as far as the village of Myerscough. The day was warm, I was equipped with a sack and the rudiments of the profession — namely a 'drum', or a tin mug, and a packet containing tea-leaves and sugar. These had been kindly given to me by Wilf who, despite thinking me a 'young mug', wished me well. He was a veteran and criminally inclined and his arguments in favour of a life of crime were tempting, but here I was on a farmer's cart with a new vista opening before my eyes. I felt like Dr Livingstone in search of undiscovered lands, the stench of poverty and the bitter resentment already leaving me as we travelled amidst fields and the distant promise of a new kind of life beyond the hills. The countryside can lay a sense of deep tranquillity in a man's heart.

The old farmer told me tales about the district and in that cart was born an interest in history and folk-lore which has never left me. I had read George Borrow and I pictured myself following in the footsteps of the great literary traveller .The romance of the road was burning brightly in the heart and soul of a young man new to its alluring call. But I was a tramp and, although I didn't fully realise it then, the so-called romance of the road is only found in books. Still, I determined to look on life as an adventure. George Borrow did his famous journeyings but once and then wrote up his experiences. I travelled my route countless times and so I write of many journeys. Mine is not a chronological account, it moves backwards and forwards in time.

I got my first drum of tea at Myerscough. I had handed my tin cup to a woman who was leaning over a cottage gate, asking her for hot water. She told me to put the tea-leaves back into my sack and to take a seat on a stool in the garden. After a while she emerged with my drum full of tea and a large slice of bread and a lump of cheese to go with it. I had learned another lesson. Never ask for tea outright for nine times out of ten people react in the same way as the old woman and you end up with a tasty snack to boot. In the tramp's every action there was this element of trickery; playing on the sentiments of the public. It was his stock-in-trade. A man boldly and unashamedly begging for a cup of tea will, more often than not, receive a rebuff, but let him do as I did and present a cup with tea already in it then he is on the right track. He simply asks for water to 'wet' his tea — after all, hikers do this. The kindliness latent in everyone (so well known to the tramp) is seduced by this approach. Let him keep his tea, is the inward reaction; poor chap, I'll make him a drink myself. Like the buttons, the elastic and the rest of the tramp's decoys, tea was an essential weapon in his armoury for piercing the soft spots of people's hearts. I very soon discovered the true character of the professional roadster, and I do not exclude myself from this generalisation: He lived off the land, off the community in general; was a con-man, a psychologist, a liar, a weaver of fiction second to none, had an inventive mind worthy of a Jules Verne on the practical side and a Sabatini on the romantic; shrewd, a flatterer, cunning, sly, not to be trusted, but was without doubt a 'type'. He was classifiable, unlike the street loafer and the pavement scrounger. He kept on the move because the law had always forced him to do so. His living was on the road and the road became a seductress, luring, beckoning, ever beckoning, and the tramp followed. For, like every other man and woman, he was always searching for that little bit of luck that might lead him who knows where.

Lancashire country dwellers are great story-tellers. The old woman pointed to a public-house, proclaiming that it was the 'Green Man' Inn. There is also a Green Man at Inglewhite, the Green Man representing the hunter who followed his craft in the forests which abounded in the area many hundreds of years ago. Now, the tree population is very sparse.

Once upon a time, began the old lady, who had seated herself on the grass amongst the wallflowers, there lived a well-to-do gentleman in the nearby village of Billsborrow. Greenhalgh by name, he was a man of influence and importance locally. One day a young chap knocked on his door. Smartly dressed, he oozed confidence as he spoke, claiming that he had arrived two days too early for a house-party at a nearby mansion. He suggested that as Mr Greenhalgh had a large residence he could put him up for a couple of nights. Greenhalgh lost his temper and told him to clear off or he would put the dogs onto him. He was having no arrogant young whipper-snapper demanding board and lodging at his house. The young fellow had no option but to lodge at the 'Green Man' public-house but, having taken exception to the manner in which Greenhalgh had sent him about his business, he racked his brains to think of some way to get his revenge. He noticed that the pub sign was very faded and suddenly his artistic eye saw the way he could get even with this local hector. He would renew the sign free of charge but alter the face of the Hunter to that of Greenhalgh! The landlord agreed to buy paint and brushes, being totally unaware of the young man's intentions. When the job was finished and the sign rehung nobody could mistake the likeness to the local firebrand. The whole district took it as a great joke, but not the butt of their laughter. Infuriated by the insult, he issued an ultimatum to the publican making it perfectly clear that if he didn't have the face changed he would see that the inn was taken off him.

I wandered on, after wishing the old lady 'Good day', the cares of the past months dropping from me as I savoured the fresh smells of the fields and the songs of the birds.

In Billsborrow I met an old chap who immediately began a tirade against the motor-car. "Since motor were invented it's bin chug-chug all day long. It was quietest village in Lancashire were Billsborrow." We were seated on the wall of a hump-backed bridge over the main Carlisle to Preston railway line.

"What about all the trains?" I asked.

"Them's only now an' then, sides, me fayther were on't railway. Dust know who was born here, lad?" I shook my head. "Why, Dicky Turner, the man who invented the word tee-total. At a temperance meeting in Preston it was."

"So, the villagers must be a very abstemious lot then," I remarked, wryly, smiling to myself as I pictured the reception that would be given to a temperance preacher in the places I visited.

The old fellow laughed heartily. "Some o't best boozers in Lancashire around here. They'd sup it out of an owd clog. Me dad was fond of his ale and so is his son. He were an engine driver, me dad. In them days the run from Preston to Lancaster — twenty miles as't crow flies — took two hours. Well on't way back train had to wait here. Station were just by t'bridge here in them days. It were in order to let trains from t'South pass as it were a single line then. Well me dad and t'fireman, owd Bill, would go down t'pub for a few pints or happen they'd pick a basket of mushrooms or two with passengers. Nobody bothered in them days, mester; they'd time to spare. Patience were a virtue then. But since motor came, well there's no patience any more, all honking and blowing and belching fumes all over't place. Trippers from 't towns what's seen no scenery before, all off on picnics to truff o'Bowland and Bleasdale. I tell thee all we got at one time were vicar on his horse and tramps. One preaching and t'other begging but I'd sooner 'ave them than motors." Although he couldn't possibly mistake me for a vicar I don't think he realised that he was talking to a tramp either.

As I walked further towards Bleasdale I could see what this soft, green country meant to the town-dweller who could afford the luxury of a 'motor'. A garden of Eden almost on the 'doorstep' of hard labour, poverty and gloom. Beacon

Fell is the perfect place for the picnickers, an ideal vantage point from which the Isle of Man is visible on a clear day. This is the site of one of Lancashire's ancient beacons. It was even known to sailors because of the white-washed farm-house just below the summit which showed up as a white speck to ships many miles out to sea. The land around the beacon, as is most of the terrain in this area, is of lush meadow and pasture land, particularly fertile in mushrooms and an enchanting array of wild plants during the Spring and Summer. Many was the time, after a night spent in a hay-shed, I made an excellent breakfast of mushrooms, gathered in the fields below the beacon. But climbing fells is not for tramps, more suited to the tourists, but I made the pilgrimage once and I must admit that the magnificent view was well worth the climb. A man can tramp for years through familiar countryside but unless he has viewed it from a height then the picture is not complete. From the summit, below me I saw the curving vale of the River Hodder, the varied changing pastoral shades of Whalley to the east, the charming market town of Clitheroe, and the witch-haunted hill of Pendle, all combining in a smiling panorama flanked to the west by the Irish Sea. To those who claim that Lancashire is a smoke-ridden country I say take a trip beyond these towns and view the green and pleasant Lancashire from the top of Beacon Fell or its mountain-mate, Parlick Hill, and then see if you still hold the view that the county Palatine is not, indeed, a very lovely one.

    Progressing northwards, there is no nicer spot than Bleasdale Moors with its lush heather studding the wild expanses in command of beautiful views, the champagne-like air and the buzzing of insects content with their lot in the perfume of gorse and heather. And to think that all this is only fifteen miles from Blackburn and twenty from Burnley. Lancashire was, and still is, the undiscovered county. I have slept away a full afternoon on the Bleasdale Moors then made my way across the bubbling Calder stream where I have drummed up on small trout caught with a cat-gut and hook baited with brandling worms. Then I have footed it through the night to put in a day's peddling in a country town.

There was a tolerable spike in this area, situated in the small town of Garstang. Its chief claim to fame is the story of a controversial character, an outspoken J.P., who turned up one cold morning at the workhouse asking for a sledgehammer. The taskmaster was astonished. "What on earth for? You are Mr Albert Simpson, J.P. aren't you, sir?"

"I am. Now, kindly give me a hammer so I can work along with these other men," he said.

"But these are tramps, sir!"

"I'm quite aware of that. Some of them don't look very strong, do they? But you wouldn't say that I was a weakling now would you? Well, we'll see how I look at the end of the task shall we." And with that he began a five-hour long assault on a pile of rocks. At the end of the task he was perspiring profusely and his hands were badly blistered and he admitted later that he wasn't fit to work manually for several days. He had proved his point.

"Then how do you expect these half-starved vagrants to do it then?" he asked at the meeting of the governors. "But it doesn't end there, you expect them to find work, then walk to the next vagrant ward for six o'clock. I tell you, gentlemen, I'm on the side of the vagrants over this. I'm a strong, well-fed man, but I was fit only for my bed afterwards. And I still feel the effects in my bones yet."

The conditions of Garstang casual ward were improved in consequence and the required quantities of stones reduced. Unfortunately, he had few supporters in his reforming campaigns. Few men were prepared to prove their points in similar fashion regarding workhouse wards. Prior to Albert Simpson's exposure of the inhuman tasks imposed on tramps those who couldn't complete the task were sent to the grimly-named Preston House of Correction as punishment for their 'crimes'.

I don't know whether he improved the tea also but they brewed a very good cup at Garstang spike when I was forced to stay the night there during a rainstorm. To get a decent cup of tea in a spike in the Twenties was indeed something special.

* * * *

The village of Scorton is a pretty gem in the green dress of the county. There is something endearing about it and I never grew tired of visiting this village; its appeal, no doubt, being further enhanced by the beauty of the immediate countryside surrounding the area. I have spent nights in Nicky Nook below the heights of Grizedale Fell and when the sun is on the narrow valley there is surely no nicer place in England. This area had several farms owned by Gentlemen Farmers in those days. The labourers lived in tied cottages and the work was made up of long hours and rewarded by very low wages. But they had work and a roof over their heads.

One day I fell into conversation with a man as he hacked at a hawthorn hedge with a scythe as I drummed up tea by the roadside. Over a cup he told me about the job and his family, he had four children. There were no fixed hours of labour, daylight to dusk was the order, with no overtime paid except for a meagre sum at haytime and harvest. When I first met him in the early Twenties he was earning twenty-seven shillings and sixpence a week, but living rent-free in a cottage which wasn't much better than a hovel. The one consolation was that he was better off than his counterparts in the south of England, but his constant threat was eviction from the cottage at a fortnight's notice if the farmer decided to sack him. Thirty-five at the outside I would have guessed his age but he looked a good ten years older. I saw a lot of farm labourers and sampled the work on a casual basis, but as a permanent job in those days it was little short of slavery. It is an old joke that farmers are always grumbling, true or not I know it is hard work to please them. The ploughman got an extra shilling or two in his wage packet and was the envy of the other labourers. Still, they seemed happy enough — people were happier with their lot than now — but I never envied these men. In fact, I heard many a one say that he envied me and that if it wasn't for the wife and kids he would join me. I met skilled farmworkers who tramped the country from job to job rather than work for one farmer.

"Do you have any time for sport?" I asked the chap at Scorton as he drank his tea, almost furtively. He was terrified of being caught taking a rest. The tea break was a thing of the future. There is a dry earthy humour about the Lancashire agriculturist.

"There's no pub in the village. That only leaves fishing and fornicating and in the Winter there's no fishing!" he said.

I went on my way, glad to be free to do as I pleased. It was on occasions such as this that I felt perfectly satisfied with my lot.

After leaving Scorton I made my way slowly through the trough of Bowland peddling my stock at farmhouses and cottages and receiving kindnesses in the form of tea and food and the hospitality of a barn for the night.

At this time it was rare indeed to meet a motor-car, but as vehicles became more popular I found it dangerous to be on the road at all, for the narrow lanes of Bowland became racing tracks for reckless and completely unskilled drivers who hadn't learned that these new toys were potentially lethal weapons. Toby Tom, an old tramping aquaintance of mine, was killed by a speeding car on one of these narrow tracks.

The wild moorland, with its bird life and ever-changing moods of colour, is a walker's delight and as I progressed northwards through this trough in the earth's structure I felt comforted by the presence of the Pennine Range flanking the right side of my route. Although my calling did not require an affinity with hills and mountains for its success, I felt their presence a safeguard on my travels. Our ancestors looked on the mountains of this land as protection against invaders, so it is little wonder that their descendants still bear this respect for these high places and the hardiest specimens amongst us feel it almost a moral obligation to visit their cloud-wreathed heights whatever the danger and discomfort. A mountaineer in the Lake District once described his climbs to me as pilgrimages of gratitude.

I recall the first time I arrived at the village of Priests Hutton. A farm track looked inviting and I followed. The stock I had purchased in Preston was gone and the need to find work was again imperative. Prepared to turn my hand to anything, I approached a group of farm buildings. My untrained eyes missed that which would have warned the experienced roadster to go no further. In my ignorance I trod the cobbles of the farmyard. About half way across, a fellow of about my own age, barely out of his teens, spotted me and his reaction was to yell "tramp" at the top of his voice, summoning a couple of men and a dog with the urgency of a bugle blast on the ear of a sleeping soldier. One had a pitchfork in his hands. Not knowing where I was heading, I fled from the yard, finding myself in a field. In front of me, about fifty yards distance, was a high fence. The dog was almost on my heels as I took off, clearing the fence in one leap. Fortunately, the fence was solid and the dog's way was barred. Now, I was in a ploughed field and, not caring what damage I might be doing, I headed in the shortest direction possible for a copse. As I reached the end of the field I looked behind me. The men had climbed the fence and one of them was pulling the dog over the top. It seemed impossible that I had cleared the obstacle whereas a dog had to be hauled over the thing — such is the strength fear lends to a man in danger of his life. In front of me now was a ditch. It seemed a simple enough leap but I had reckoned without the heavy soil clinging to my boots, and the toll of my energy taken by the run. I landed in the middle of the ditch and sank up to my neck in a heavy substance. The dogs howls served to force me out of the morass and I made my leaden way to the shelter of the trees where I lay low in a clump of bracken. The stink was abominable. I had fallen in a ditch full of pig manure. I hope the reader will excuse a terrible pun if I say that the foul stuff saved my bacon! The dog lost my scent and scurried away in another direction.

6

KIRKBY LONSDALE

No gutter-snipe, however lowly, could ever have felt so utterly contemptible as I did when I entered the town of Kirkby Lonsdale. In the lanes and fields I was away from the public gaze, but once in the town I was an affront to human decency. I reached the town more by accident than design, this tramp-town which was to become my favourite calling place on the road. But entering it for the first time I had no idea where to call for help, if help there was to be had. I had attracted all manner of flies and insects like the proverbial jam pot, a walking feast for the pests. The stink was nauseating and people were giving me a wide berth. I stopped one old chap to ask him the way to the casual ward. It was my only hope in the circumstances. Placing one hand over his nose, he pointed with the other. I found it on Mill Brow and discovered that a most unusual arrangement existed, the workhouse and the common lodging-house being in the same building. I knocked on a door and asked if it was the casual ward. A woman opened it and immediately staggered back in disgust.

"Ye'll not be coming in here, so ye won't? Is it pigs ye've been with? It's over yonder ye'll be wanting but, God knows, ye'll not be welcome!" She had pointed to a comfortable-looking house along the lane. Here, I found a man who told me he was the relieving officer for the district. Standing well back so as not to offend his nostrils too severely, he smiled as he listened to the tale of my flight from the farm. He said, "You'll need some new togs, lad. Here, take this to the old clothes shop. She'll fit you out." He handed me a chit on which he had written, 'Kindly supply with clothes.' "First of all, you'll need a dip in the river, you don't exactly smell like a rose garden. Come on, and I'll see what we can do."

I walked with him to the workhouse. I waited outside and shortly he came out with a garment like a shroud made of sacking, and a dirty mackintosh. He told me to go into a shed and leave my clothes there. He would set fire to them later. Clad in the sack and the mac, he led me down to the River Lune where he pointed out a safe place for a dip.

"I hope there's none of the local spinsters watching," he joked as I bathed in the nude.

After the welcome plunge, I again donned the coverings and set off to follow my guide's directions to the old clothes shop. The woman there was only too glad to do business, for she was sure of her money – a lot of her trade being done on 'tick.' I was a new man right down to a pair of shoddy, but comfortable, brown boots. The tweed jacket had that shabby-genteel look about it, so popular with the gentry in those days, but the corduroy trousers looked as if they had been on familiar terms with the corpulent backside of a farmer, for the seat had been widened by the addition of a leather patch and I must have looked like a circus clown. But they were trousers and, with the aid of string and a pair of braces I found in a bin, they did me excellent service for several months.

I felt that I owed the official a word of thanks, so I went back to his house, but by this time a queue of tramps had formed at his door. I listened in fascination to the many and varied hard-luck stories these fellows voiced. But each one was given a chit and no questions asked and no money changed hands. Some of the chits were for the lodging-house and some for the bus to Kendal. One man had a dog and, with typical canine unconcern for person or property, it urinated on the officer's trousers, wetting him down one leg. This normally placid man gave vent to his feelings, making it clear in choice language that he didn't take kindly to being used as a lamp post. Wherever men of the road gathered there was always a wag and fortunately there was one in the queue. "Don't be too hard on Rover, mister," he piped up. "After all, you are the relieving officer!" Whereupon the officer burst out laughing and gave the dog-owner his chit.

It was no use me asking for a chit for the lodging-house as I had no money for food. It was the workhouse if I wanted to eat. I joined the queue outside the workhouse and at six o'clock we were admitted and got our ration of bread and marg., with a mug of tea to wash it down. This was the best spike I ever visited and it was known far and wide as a 'Good night's doss.' There was fresh hot water and decent towelling and a padded sacking mattress to sleep on.

It was in the kip room that I fell into conversation with a tramp who, judging by his voice, could have been a teacher of elocution for he was softly spoken, obviously well educated and possessed the finest delicate pair of hands I had ever seen on a man. He told me that he had visited every town and village in Britain with a Market Cross and that the one in Kirkby was a replica of the cross in Malmesbury in Wiltshire. "Some day I might write a book or a thesis on these crosses," he told me, adding confidentially, "Start talking culture here and they think you are some kind of intellectual crack-pot. Still, I suppose I am." He laughed softly. He was obviously pleased with my interest and confided in me when he could see that I was a good listener. "What a treat to meet someone who takes an interest in nature. These chaps tramp the same country as I do yet they don't see the same things. Talk about birds and the moods of nature and they haven't any answer. But, you see, I was brought up in the country before I went up to Oxford. Yes, I know what you are thinking — 'What the hell is an Oxford man doing in a spike?' It's a natural question, I'll grant you that. After graduation I took a Tutor's post in Somerset. Chap rolling in money, big tycoon somewhere in the City — you know the type. Well, he had three sons who were strangers to him; he hardly bothered with them. I taught them for a year or so and went with them on rambles and played cricket and went horse-riding. Things he should have been doing. But he also had a lovely wife. The fellow was a swine, an arrogant self-opinionated blackguard and he treated his wife like a skivvy. Well, you've guessed the rest, I suppose. It's not a new yarn. You'll read the same stuff in any shilling novelette, I don't doubt. She and I fell in love and had a clandestine affair. Of course there's always someone to spill the beans; this time, a young groom who was no doubt jealous. I was thrown out physically by a couple of his staff in simply the clothes I stood up in. I daren's go back, lacked back-bone, I suppose. Well, I drifted like a love-lorn fool, wandered and simply walked from place to place. I tried for a couple of Tutor's posts but I'd no references, you see. Not that I tried very hard, I'd got to like the casual life — that was the trouble. It's fifteen years ago now and I'm an unashamed tramp. Not an uplifting tale, is it? Of course, normal society will say I've wasted my talents, but I don't know. Does one have to follow the well-trodden accepted path in life?"

He was not only an engaging speaker, he was a good listener also — not a common combination I have found. He listened with interest to my tale of the chase at Priests Hutton and when he had heard me out he said, "Didn't you notice anything on the wall that leads to the farm?"

"You know it then?" I asked.

"I'll say I do. That place is notorious. They hate tramps. Didn't you see marks on the wall?"

I suddenly remembered some drawings I had seen. "I did see some childish marks," I said.

"Childish marks! Not quite, young fellow. If you had known your tramp-lore you might have saved yourself a bath in the pig muck. That farm is a bad mark. The sign I chalked on the wall — three times for emphasis — was like a barred gate. See." He chalked on the kip-room wall with a piece of white stone — "That means danger. Keep out at all costs. I passed the very place only a couple of days ago and renewed the marks. So you had better learn your lessons, my friend."

Needless to say, I soon became familiar with the tribal signs used by tramps. Mostly they were used by country tramps and rarely seen in towns. The most common ones were as follows:

LIST OF SIGNS

Very hospitable. (very commonly used)

No good. (very commonly used)

Dangerous!

Kind lady.

Beware Dog! (Some signs show dog)

Keep out!

Woman with children.

Afraid of tramps.

Use hard-luck story.

Fruit trees worth raiding. (rare sign)

Police house.

Foreigners live here.

Will provide work.

Go east or west but not here!

Phones for police!

Danger — ex-warder in gaol.

Too many tramps call. (Always safe)

Church people.

Sandwiches, cakes given.

Night's kip here.

Sick people. Be understanding.

Women only. Be careful not to alarm.

Believes all vagrants should be in prison. Don't call.

Keep out!

Good for brew. (This is not in common use. Have seen it once and is probably the mark of one tramp)

*   *   *   *

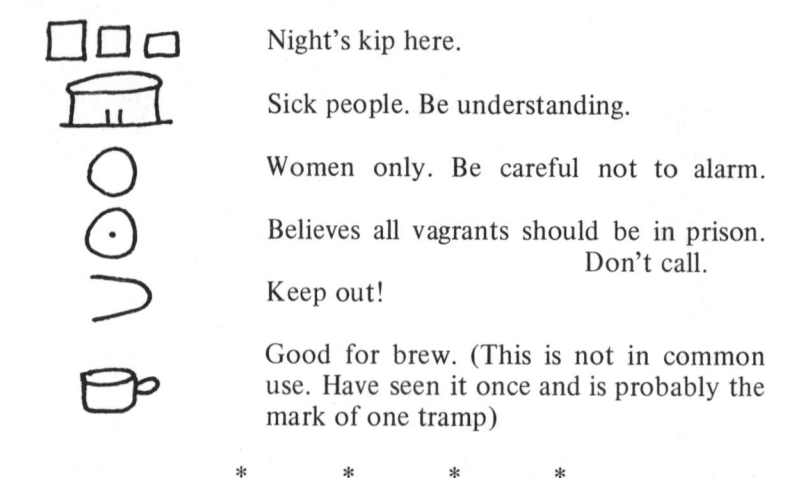

In the morning we were wakened by a gong. In fact, it was a tin can beaten by a stick by the tramp-major, a man who was known as 'Jack Specs' on account of the large spectacles he wore. He shot back the bolt of the ward door and shouted, "Come out, you bloodhounds!" We were led out into the task yard where we were confronted by a pile of River Lune cobbles. These had to be knapped for road mending. Knapping is hard work and our task was to fill a wheel-barrow apiece before we were free to go. These cobbles were used for remetalling the roads.

'Specs' was a human sort of chap and I became quite friendly with him over the years. Fond of a drink, he was one of the real characters of the little market town and once he spread a rumour that he was shortly coming into money. A rich uncle in the States was dying and Jack would be on the receiving end of a fat bequest. The tale spread from pub to pub and in every one the rich-man-to-be was treated to drinks wherever he went. Suddenly he was seen in a new light by people who had never deigned to speak to him before. But the make-believe legacy never came and Jack was found out to be spinning a yarn. His new-found friends left him as quickly as he had acquired them.

Many colourful characters collected at Kirkby. In the Twenties, particularly, it was a town of great personality and attracted all manner of showmen and pedlars. Before the First World War travelling German bands were constant visitors to English towns and I heard many stories of the wonderful musicianship of these men. So it was something of a surprise when, several years after the end of the war, I listened to a recital given by one of these bands in the Market Place at Kirkby. Their rendering of German opera was quite beautiful. They all stopped at the lodging-house run by MacFarlanes, an Irish family, before catching the morning train to Kendal. To come over to England took a lot of courage and, indeed, turned into a foolhardy expedition. After the recital one of the fiddlers said something in broken English to a boy. The lad laughed only to be rudely pulled away by his mother. "Don't speak to that pig!" she shouted. "He's the chap who killed your father." It was sad. The German bands never came again to England and were never replaced for colour and stirring music.

A superb showman, known as 'Fetch the ladder', was a regular visitor to all the Lakeland towns and I have never seen a finer show from a street performer. In a narrow Kirkby street, where a mistake could have cost him dearly in broken shop windows, he would balance a wheel on his chin, then calling out "Fetch the ladder, Mary" he would sink to his knees whilst the faithful Mary placed the bottom rung of the ladder on the top of the wheel. Slowly rising to his feet, he would keep them both balanced until he was on tip-toes. The gasps of admiration for the feat would be tempered by the fear that, at any second, the ladder would topple. It never did. As a final act, he would throw potatoes high into the air and split them when they landed on his bald head.

One night over drum-up at MacFarlanes, he confided in me that he had been a member of a Family Music-Hall Act until, in his quest for drink, he absconded with the week's takings. He met Mary on the road and they toured the towns together and made a reasonable living out of it.

Another colourful character was 'Chalky Bill', a resident of the town and a respected citizen despite his reputation for eccentricity. 'Chalky' was an inventor who had improved the shuttle for a well-known firm of sewing-machine manufacturers. In gratitude for this, they appointed him as their

Service and Sales Agent for the County of Westmorland. He was noted for 'button-holing' people in the street and demanding chalk. I remember one occasion when he grabbed the lapel of my jacket and asked, "Esta bita chalk, Lad?" I produced a whitestone from my pocket. "Ta, I want to show thee a new invention o'mine lad," and he proceeded to chalk an intricate diagram on a carved oak door. Above us was a sign bearing the name of a well-known bank. 'Chalky' didn't care what he chalked on and it was said that his queer drawings could be seen all over the district. When I knew him he was an old man and the last time I saw him he was riding a three-wheeler bike over the Devil's Bridge, which crossed the Lune, a pet raven perched on his shoulders. The local barber wrote a poem about the eccentric and it was pinned on his wall for many years. Unfortunately, I can only remember half of it:

'Chalky' was a man of ingenious turn of mind.
He dabbled in inventions of a highly novel kind.
The only thing that troubled him was just the trifling fact,
That none of his inventions were ever known to act.
He made a clockwork pussy that couldn't catch a mouse,
An automatic fire alarm that set fire to the house . . .

and so, in similar vein.

Jonty Wilson's blacksmith's shop was the parliament of Kirkby. Those of us who had stopped at MacFarlanes would buy what we could afford for breakfast then go to the forge where Jonty had a fire set aside for our use for half-an-hour every morning. There, we would have a frizzle of bacon and a brew of tea and join in the general conversation. And what a motley collection of characters would assemble there and what strange yarns I heard. I remember particularly a defrocked parson, known as Ebenezer, who would always insist we said Grace before our breakfast, but Captain Barney was the best yarn-spinner of them all. As a story-teller I never met his equal and though I met hundreds of street singers and every kind of busker, he was the only street raconteur I encountered. He would attract a crowd like a soap-box orator, but instead of spouting politics or religion at them he would tell them stories, enhanced with theatrical gestures and a sense of drama which couldn't have been bettered by a professional actor. A born raconteur, he told me how he had left his ship at Glasson Dock to go on a wild drinking spree that lasted nearly a week. When he returned his ship had sailed. Rum was his downfall. He told us how, when sailing home from North Africa, millions of Painted Ladies — the butterfly variety — settled on the sails of the vessel causing it to keel over. He claimed to be an expert on the migratory habits of butterflies and carried with him a collapsible butterfly-net which he had purchased from a pawnbroker. I have since discovered that this species of butterfly does come from North Africa and I have seen all he told us verified in books on the subject of lepidoptery. Red Admirals and Clouded Yellows also travelled this way in the days of sail. It was a comical sight to see him in Captain's cap and ragged clothes running across the Fells with his net in pursuit of butterflies. When he had caught them he would mount them in books and sell them to dealers in Kendal. He had a most compelling way of holding an audience, born out of the fact that he was relating first-hand stories. One which he could really enrich with overtones of melodrama and sinister eastern voices was the tale of a friend who had owned a tin mine in Australia. One night his friend suspected robbers and paid a surprise visit to the ore workings. He surprised a Chinaman who was filling a bag with ore. The Oriental hurled a hammer but it missed its mark and the mine-owner felled him with a swipe of his hand, killing him. He was tried for murder but acquitted. The affair had been such an ordeal that in order to try to forget it he went out on a hunting trip alone and got lost. He was found a week later, a skeleton left by the white ants who had eaten his flesh. Real creepy horror tales were his speciality and his audiences enjoyed them and paid him well for his entertainment.

Although I thoroughly enjoyed Captain Barney's immense repertoire of tales, there have been long, lonely nights when I have recalled to mind the gruesome details of his yarns and found myself shivering in a barn, or under a bridge by some remote river, shivering not with cold but with fear and resolving never again to listen to the captain's tales of adventure. But I couldn't resist them. He was a great entertainer and a loss to the stage for I have never met his equal in the line of dramatic story telling. He was found dead in a hen shed near Skipton, an inconspicuous end for a man who had lived so romantically in his seafaring days and was so well liked when down on his luck.

Another visitor to Jonty's forge was the 'Doc' who told tales of medical life in East Africa. He recounted how he had been called out to attend to two natives who had run amok trying to kill one another. One, he found, had had his abdomen split by a spear, the other had a nasty gash in the thigh. Thinking he was a 'gonner', he started on the thigh wound. Whilst thus engaged, a native 'wizard' arrived with his assistant and immediately got to work on the other patient. Among his 'tools' was a bottle containing big brown ants of the fighting kind with horned heads as big as a grain of wheat and armed with mandibles which opened like pincers when anything was presented to them. These were put to practical use during the operation. The 'surgeon' drew the pierced stomach together and his assistant held together the two edges of the tear. The wizard then took an ant and presented it to the edges which it bit through with its mandibles. Immediately its head was nipped off by the 'surgeon' and the skin remained fixed. It was the first stitch of the sewing up said the 'Doc' and he proceeded to put between twenty and thirty along the tear. Eventually, these would be absorbed like cat gut. The remarkable part about the operation was the self-control of the patients who, although conscious, made no sound. Both recovered in a surprisingly short time. He had never revealed how he had come to be living as a tramp. In fact, I couldn't believe that he really had been a doctor until, one day, I saw him examining a sick man in a lodging-house. There was no doubting the skill and expertise and when the local doctor arrived his diagnosis was a confirmation of the one reached by the 'Doc'. "You are a doctor, aren't you?" said the local man. "I was," answered the tramp and that was the end of the conversation.

Many years later I was told by a lodging-house owner that the 'Doc' had confided in him when he was drunk and told him that he had practised in London but had been struck off the Medical Register for performing illegal abortions.

I met such a diversity of characters that I find it impossible to recall them all to mind from the dark recesses of memory. Pathetic and comical. tragic and bizarre, the full spectrum of human life was to be found.

I first met Ikey Fitzgibbons in Kirkby Lonsdale. Ikey sold dogs, but not his own and was a born yarn spinner, which is a polite way of saying he was a prolific liar. He was one of those people who tell so many lies they begin to believe them themselves. Like most tramps he was an avid hoarder of string; he was always begging or stealing it. Ikey always had string in his pocket. String is a very useful commodity on the road — invaluable for securing newspaper to your legs and body, for shoe laces and so on — but Ikey used his for dog leads. He simply picked out a decent-looking dog, put the string round its neck, led it to some district some distance from where he found it and then knocked on house doors until he found a buyer. He was a born actor. Always, he was down on his luck, had to leave the district urgently in order to commence work in a strange town. He dare not think of leaving his poor dog all alone — always, he sold his dog. His graft was a precarious one and business transactions were not always without snags for fate played Ikey a cruel blow in Kirkby. He knocked on a door and told the usual story. The man sympathised, or so it seemed, then went off to talk it over with 'the family', who turned out to be two policemen. Fido belonged to the man's brother. Ikey had timed it to a nicety and was in time for the morning Petty Sessions.

Butty Done was an eccentric. A 'crank' who, if one of fate's many signposts had directed him along the lanes of respectable citizenship instead of the midden-path of poverty, would have been labelled an amiable buffoon or a 'mad professor', a welcome addition to the social life of the golf club. In centuries gone by he would have been hailed toast of the Coffee-houses in cravat, ruffles and powdered wig, delighting the toffs and toadies with his whimsicalities, an eccentric amongst eccentrics. But Butty was a tramp, was put in the lunatic asylum and branded 'madman.' Some of his antics, it has to be admitted, were odd, like lathering up his face with soap by using the doss-house dog's tail as a shaving brush. Then there was his habit of addressing himself to trees and inanimate objects. One day I accompanied him from Kirkby as far as Kendal. Being a very tall man, he forgot to duck his head and so cracked it against a low canopy outside a flower-shop. He proceeded to lay about the offending wooden structure with a stick, addressing it thus: "Must the inanimate object be free from pain? Take that, sir — and that!" When a policeman arrived on the scene, Butty proceeded to give him a lecture on the unfairness of a world where inanimate objects can feel no pain yet inflict it upon humans who can. G.K. Chesterton would have lionised him for literary posterity whilst Cervantes would have recognised a serious rival to Don Quixote. Windmill-tilting by a man who wears not the shining armour of the knights of old but a ragged tail-coat with a newspaper cummerbund is not condoned outside popular novels. Last time I heard of Butty he was confined to a cell. God knows what that was like. He wandered, had tendencies to go off and not come back, you see. What oafs were they who expected a tramp to remain stationary?

Carlisle Kate was a manageress in a large fashion shop frequented by the 'county' set. She was tempted to steal, succumbed and ended up in prison. On her release her two sisters had left the house where all three had lived, having sold up and moved away without leaving a forwarding address. And so an empty house greeted her when she left prison, her own flesh and blood were too ashamed to continue to live with her. She received one-third of the sale-price but her prison record was against her and work was unobtainable and so the money soon drained away. Like so many others, she made the old mistake of thinking that work would be easier to find in another town. It wasn't. The road beckoned and she survived by begging food and doing farm work whenever there was a chance of a job. One day a tractor knocked her down on a lane in Westmorland. She died of her injuries. Her story was revealed in the newspapers, a minor sensation about a one-time highly respected business woman. She was given a pauper's funeral with only two tramps to mourn her passing. A beautiful floral tribute in the form of a cross was placed by one on the newly-covered grave. With his friend, he had stolen the flowers from the local park and, together, they had sat up half the night in a Kendal doss-house making the wreath. Kate retained her dignity to the end and would never mix with other tramps, male or female. It is amazing how some people can retain their pride even when they are at life's lowest level. I call them the 'How the mighty are fallen brigade.' They are tramps to everyone but themselves.

The popular myth with many people was that all tramps were dangerous characters. I soon became well used to people crossing over to the other side of the street at my approach, children were called into the house by their parents and old ladies held their umbrellas at the ready. My back and legs still bear the marks of dog-bites and all because I had walked past a house or a farm. 'Set the dog on him' is an expression not unknown to my ears. I have met violent tramps but they were in no greater proportion to violent men in other walks of life. Tramps have murdered, raped, maimed, committed arson and blackmail – but so have doctors, lawyers, bankers and racehorse trainers. Most tramps simply wanted to be left alone. I know tramps who, as far as I was aware, were completely honest men. Most were petty criminals, if you counted the 'arch' sins of stealing turnips, poaching and obtaining money under false pretences as crimes, whilst business men were robbing and cheating daily in the name of fair commerce. Wash, clothe and 'dicky up' a tramp, seat him behind a city desk and he would have become an honest rogue. Many kinds of flotsam inhabited the doss-houses, but none more likeable than the navvies. Irish, for the most part, they were teak-hard men yet often with hearts as soft as putty. I have received many kindnesses from navvies. Their biggest downfall was drink. Huge bruisers of men, capable of long hours of digging and shovelling, then marches of teens of miles across country in search of more work, they were to be admired. Often they would get wildly drunk and end up in prison. As a class they kept to themselves and deeply resented the title 'tramp' if anyone was foolish enough to confer it upon them. In Kirkby a navvy vomited on the kitchen floor. One of the lodgers called him a filthy tramp. The navvy felled him with one almighty swipe with his spade-like hand, cutting a long wound in the side of his head then walked out of the house and round the corner to give himself up to a policeman. Such was the stigma of the word tramp to some men.

There were women tramps on the road, often in cahoots with men tramps living as man and wife in those doss-houses which condoned this sort of thing. There were men and women on the road who were the bastards of this road-lust (call it what you will), brought up on the road; families travelling together, wheeling their belongings around in old perambulators. They were quite common sights in the Kirkby area and treated kindly by the farmers who gave them work. I once met a woman tramp who stole bicycles and rode from doss-house to doss-house, here the machine was usually stolen by another lodger and she simply stole another machine — and so it went on.

Colourfully dressed French onion sellers were a very common sight before the war as, festooned with onions, they rode the road on bicycles. One foolish 'froggie' came to the doss-house in Kirkby where he naively left his bike outside and his clothes on top of his bed and his entire stock of onions underneath it. You will have guessed the result of this foolish man's actions. A French-bereted English onion seller — whose only French was 'wee-wee monsewer' — was pedalling furiously away from the town when the foreigner awoke to his distress. He cried like a bereaved child and was forced to dress in the only clothes available, the dirty rags of the man who had stolen his stock-in-trade. In return for French onions he received English fleas.

We were all welcomed at Kirkby, especially at Jonty's forge and no questions were asked. The Smithy was an integral part of rural life, as English as the wicket at Lord's or a swoop of wild geese on a Lakeland tarn. There was something intimately poetical about the Smithy as the red-hot sparks were scattered by the beefy arms of the Smith; the invigorating tang of burning hoof and the clear ring of metal upon metal. It ranked second only to the inn as a place where men could come together to talk about everything under the sun, from the price of cattle food to the vicar's attractive wife.

One morning, whilst we were preparing breakfast over the fire, a tweedy-looking man came in for a chat with the

Blacksmith. There was no doubting his obvious superiority as far as position and education went, but there was a friendliness about the man which the presence of tramps didn't dampen. He gave us all a hearty 'Good morning' and a sixpence apiece. He was Lord Lonsdale of the enormous cigars and the famous boxing belt.

The Vale of Lune and Kirkby Lonsdale have been immortalised in words by Ruskin and in oils by Turner. The view from St. Mary's Church — the town's name comes from the old name — is worth travelling a long way to see and is known as 'Ruskin's View'. From this spot a magnificent view of the Lune, weaving its course at the foot of Casterton Fells, is seen. It would take a Dickens to paint a pen-picture of the characters who, over the years, helped to add colour to everyday life in the town. They accepted the odd and the curious in Kirkby and those of us who were classed in this category of life's characters were glad of it.

7

SINGING AND POACHING

It was on the road leading into Kirkby Lonsdale from Casterton that I was frightened by a monkey. One doesn't expect to meet a monkey bounding down an English road. The day was hot and with the desire for a mug of tea very strong in my thoughts, I had decided to try the very next house with my drum and a new line of leather laces. I had learned by experience that ordinary shoe-laces were no use to country folk. The creature leaped along a dry stone wall as I increased my pace for I had heard the 'Doc' tell tales of terrible diseases caused by the bites of wild animals. I crossed to the other side of the road and espying a five-barred gate was soon astride it, but I would have been as hard pressed trying to lose my own shadow for the monkey sprang up beside me.

"He won't hurt you, mate." I was relieved to hear a human voice. A little chap, wearing a brown bowler hat and clad in a bizarre patchwork suit of multi-coloured materials whistled to the monkey. He hadn't a tooth visible in his head. He beckoned me to join him, where I found he was making tea in a field. A hurdy-gurdy cart was parked by the roadside. "Sambo won't hurt you, mate," said the little chap. This was the first non-Italian 'Gurdy' man I had met and it was rather unique for an Englishman to be in this business. He gave me a check-over with his eyes then asked in a lisping manner: "D'you sing mate?"

"As a matter of fact, I do."

"What are yar, a bwarry-tone? Judging by yar build I'd say as yar was."

"I'd say so," I agreed.

"Yes, a bwarry-tone, I'd say. Well, we'll soon see, Mate." Then, looking at me hard, he added, "Ain't a gwiddler are yar? Them wailing willies what sing hymns ain't no use."

"No, I only sing if there's accompaniment. I've busked on Morecambe sands with a minstrel troop," I informed him.

"You 'as?" He looked quite impressed as he threw a handful of tea leaves into the bubbling drum. "I don't wike gwiddlers. Wailers they are — mind yar, it's every man to his twade I say. It don't pay to sing good on the streets it don't. Sound wike a cove what's got wargitis and they'll give yar a threepenny dodger to bugger off. If Caruso sang on the street he wouldn't make it pay. No, you has to be wough, mate — dead wough." He was winding up the hurdy-gurdy and when that was finished he poured tea into my drum and from the compartment at the back of the contraption produced milk and sugar. That cupboard was like Aladdin's cave, containing all manner of knick-knacks.

"What a wonderful way to travel," I remarked, marvelling at this self-contained way of travelling and making a living.

"It's been my life for twenty years, mate. I'm Syd, by the way. What's your moniker, mate?"

"Joe," I said, and we shook hands.

"Wight, Joe, I says you is a bwarry-tone. Nar sup yar tea and let's 'ear yar warble a stave or two. Pass the audition and I'll give yar a job in Kirkby. I'm wooking for a singer see. Since I wost me teeth I can't sing no more. Fifty-fifty on the collection — game?"

"I'm game alright, but what's the song?"

"Wand of Hope and gwory."

That was a stroke of luck for I knew it well from childhood days in the school choir. He moved a lever then started to wind the gurdy. This time it produced a honky-tonk sound and once the melody got under way, after a laborious start, I sang a few bars of the chorus. Syd was delighted. "You'll do, mate. You is a bwarry-tone — up, Sambo." The monkey jumped on top of the contraption then off we set down the winding lane into the town.

As we walked he told me about his experiences in Lancashire. The depression of the early thirties was at its height and he had been touring the mill towns with the hurdy-gurdy, sleeping in brick kilns at night. Such a precious instrument wouldn't have lasted long on the doss-house circuit. Unfortunately Syd had met with a poor reception in the towns, particularly Blackburn. The cotton towns had suffered badly.

"Yar see, this 'ere gurdy onwy plays two toons – Choppings Polly-nase and Wand of Hope and Gwory. Well, one's too highbrow for working folk and t'other ain't no good just now. It's stuck, see? Keeps playing them two toons and no others, weckon it's for the scrap yard. Me reppy-tower is wather wimited, see: that's why I want a singer, see. But I'll warn yar, Wand of Hope and Gwory is a dangerous song in England just now – werry dangerous."

"Dangerous?" I said. "How do you make that out?"

"Scout's honour, mate. I was pwaying it in Blackburn last week when I gets surrounded be a crowd as looked like a lynching mob. Outside a pub it was. There was hunger in their eyes, mate. I saw it. One bwoke starts yelling at me, 'Where's the bloody hope and there ain't no gwory being on the streets out of work, mate.' 'Mother of the frigging free!' yells another cove. 'Ruddy insult that is, mate. Move yar bleedin' barrer or we'll move it for yer.'" Syd stopped the cart and wiped his brow with a red handkerchief. "It was a bwoody daft toon to play to bwokes what's got wives and children what they can't feed, weren't it, mate?"

"Well, I'm glad you've warned me," I said. "But though times are bad everywhere I don't think you'll find it as bad in the country places. There's poverty everywhere, but somehow it's more obvious in the towns."

"That's what I'm hoping, mate. I ain't trundled this old groaner all this way for nuttin'. Come on, mate, and sing up woud and cwear – me, you and Sambo here are going to do well – I can feel it in me bones." He spun his brown bowler into the air and caught it with the agility of a juggler. It was obvious that Syd was an experienced travelling showman of many parts.

After a lot of bustling and pushing, we managed to reach a clear space outside the 'Royal' hotel. The market-day crowds were in happy mood as they bartered and bought at the stalls in the Square; sheep, cows, pigs and dogs all mingled together in what seemed to me a colossal scrimmage, but the Fell farmers knew their own animals and, every now and then, some of them would be picked out and herded together as they were sold to the accompaniment of piercing voices and the slapping together of hands. The pubs were doing fine trade and so, too, were the pedlars and the street performers. Market-days were great events then, and almost every country town in the land had one; the quacks and the stall-holders moved around in a circuit and the tramps followed. They were the little fish swimming in the wake of the big fish. When the weather grew cold and winter took over many moved into the larger towns, away from the countryside; and the tramp followed, parasitic to the last, a camp-follower of the main attractions, cashing in on the large assemblies.

Places were often at a premium on Fair days and when we edged our 'gurdy' into the space several tramp-phoneys had to push up to give us room. The 'Doc' gave me a cheery grin. He was peddling corn cure which he made up in the lodging-house by boiling up herbs on the stove and blending them with leaf lard. 'Doc's Corn-salve' became quite famous in the Lake District and Lunesdale. Another tramp, who was peddling cough candy, gave us a dirty look and slouched away. We had timed our arrival well for the smallholders and farmers were receptive to music, most having downed a few pints to wash away the dust and fatigue of an early morning start and many were quite intoxicated and, with any luck, we were in for a good collection. Syd was the only gurdy man in town and after I had sung the introduction and the first rousing chorus, people were joining in with gusto — 'Land of Hope and Glory, Mother of the Free . . . !'

We received an enthusiastic ovation. "You're on to a winner there, lads," shouted the 'Doc', interrupting his 'There is no need to limp any more, ladies!' routine. Pennies were thrown broadcast on the cobbles and retrieved by Sambo who was an expert at the task. After this he went round with Syd's brown bowler, much to the delight of the kids. His dance routine on top of the 'gurdy' to 'Choppings Polly-nase' brought us further applause and more money.

We repeated the success three times and with the sun beating down it was hot work.

"Fwancy a gargle?" Syd lisped after a couple of hours of performing. I was quick to agree. Market day in Kirkby meant all-day licensing hours, so we made our way to a small pub where the landlord tolerated tramps as long as they didn't cause trouble. He was a good friend and would sometimes give me a piece of his wife's homemade meat pie. The crafty 'Doc' followed, knowing we were in funds. In the tiny 'Snug' room of the pub we counted our takings and split the money between us. Four shillings and sixpence each, making a total of nine shillings raked in by the recital. This was exceptional for a busking session, a small fortune to a tramp who was used to counting his wealth in pennies and not shillings. We stood the 'Doc' a couple of pints and, naturally enough, he encouraged us warmly to form ourselves into a double act, but sticking to the country towns. The world seemed rosy. It often does after a few pints.

Syd agreed to go with me to the Miss Whittakers' house which was a good four miles walk but, with the two of us trundling the cart, the miles soon sped by. For the first time in many a long month I was quite tipsy. But after a wash in a beck to sober up and a drum up of sweet black tea I felt in a fit state to call on the ladies with the button card. I knew they wouldn't be in the market for leather laces, but the younger sister's eyes lit up in delight when she saw the Hurdy-Gurdy. Syd kept a tight hold on Sambo in case he went in search of a chicken dinner or a duck supper, for the yard was full of poultry.

"I'm all right for buttons," said the younger Miss Whittaker politely. "But I'll tell you what, if you'll play the Hurdy-Gurdy I'll give you tea and cake in exchange and you can both use the old barn – but you'll make sure the monkey is tied up won't you?" She eyed Sambo rather nervously. I rooted in my sack and handed her a box of matches and a pipe. This was the code of the road as far as tramps went, the unwritten understanding between them and the owners of barns and sheds. Many folk insisted on a search – not that I blamed them – for the dangers, not to mention the loss of property, were very obvious.

"Do you smoke?" she asked Syd, kindly.

"No, marm," he lied, for he had smoked a couple of Woodbine's whilst we were in the public house. I didn't want to show him up as a liar in front of her so I said nothing. Syd then started to wind the hurdy-gurdy and we were joined by the elder sister. Both were greatly amused by Sambo's antics and rewarded us well with a large jug of tea and a plate piled high with cheese sandwiches. Tea brewed in a jug is an old Northern custom which is well worth preserving. We ate our meal in the yard and were then let into the barn by the ladies who locked it behind us. Syd was impressed at first.

"By the hell, mate, you haven't half got a good cwib here. You'll be marrying into the famiwy next, what yer say, Sambo?"

"Yes and I want to stay welcome, see. Now tie this animal up and hand over that packet of Woodbine's and the matches. You can't smoke in here."

At that he began to turn nasty. "Now wook here, mate, if I wants to smoke I'll smoke, see. Wocked in a barn at seven o'clock what the hell else is there to do, eh? Bugger them two women I'm having a dwag, see."

"I got you in here so you'll keep 'em in your pocket," I said.

In answer he took a cigarette from the packet and struck a match which I knocked from his hand. It was a foolish move on my part. Immediately the tinder-dry straw caught fire.

"You stupid bugger," roared the Gurdy man and in seconds we were rolling on the floor fighting. That fight probably saved our lives for the flames were extinguished by our bodies and we weren't even singed, but the smoke was suffocating us as we banged furiously on the door to be let out. The women were very annoyed and said we had betrayed their confidence. I was told never to call again otherwise I would be reported to the police.

It was the end of a promising partnership and made me resolve to be very careful in future before joining up with a fellow traveller along the road. But worse than that, I had lost the best calling place I have ever had in all my years on the road and that to a tramp was a tragedy. Syd, Sambo and the Gurdy went back towards Kirkby Lonsdale and I headed for Kendal sleeping out on the Fells.

It has always been my experience that once hard luck strikes it quickly has another thrust. The next morning, feeling stiff and cold after a night in the bracken, I walked a couple of miles to a farm-house where I knew tramps were welcomed. When I reached the yard the farmer met me and I could tell immediately that I wasn't welcome. I had carefully checked for warning chalk signs, but there were none.

"You can clear off and tell the rest of 'em to keep away," he said. As he was holding a pitch fork rather menacingly I didn't argue.

Down the lane I met a young labourer. "No luck, mate?" he asked.

"I can't understand it. What's happened?"

"Why, a tramp come only yesterday and asks at the door for summat. Farmer's missus give him a barm cake and a lump of cheese. Well, when she'd closed the door he chucks it over a wall and shouts, 'that's no good for buying beer.' Gaffer heard him and threatened to run him through with his pitch fork. Put him right off tramps. I reckon as you is unlucky, mate."

I found out later that the tramp who had 'spoiled a good mark' was Frank, the tramp, as this morose, unfriendly man was known to everyone.

I met some unlikeable men on the pad, but Frank was detestable. He gave tramps a bad name. Such a statement might seem an absurdity but, generally speaking, tramps had a good name with country folk. The craft of the tramp was one of his major weapons. No matter how big a rogue he was he would put on a front of decency when calling on houses and farms. In this way tramps became accepted as harmless wanderers who simply required a cup of tea or somewhere to sleep. And so the title 'Gentlemen of the Road' was conferred upon them and has persisted to this day when elderly people look back with nostalgia and affection for the tramps they knew in their youth. Now many of my contemporaries were decent enough people but to consider them as 'gentlemen' was going too far; yet it was a title gratefully accepted by the tramp and upheld even by the biggest rogues amongst us; so the experienced roadster knew when he was well off, and he played up to the role expected of him by the public.

But not so Frank. He was a blight on common decency; a man with no saving graces and detested by his fellow tramps. There is a most unlikely, but true, tale concerning him which was told in Lunesdale for many years. I recall him as an outright beggar with no subtlety, a large-framed man who always walked with his head bent forward, hands clutched tightly behind his back. Winter and Summer he wore a long black coat tied in the middle with a string. Occasionally, out of sheer desperation, he would take a job threshing for a Lunesdale farmer. I didn't like the man and was rather disgusted to find him working next to me in the field. At dinner time the farmer's wife invited all the labourers into the kitchen for a meal and made no distinction between tramps and none tramps. Knowing full well the pangs of hunger, it always annoys me to see food left on plates, but I wouldn't have had the nerve, or the cheek, to do what Frank did. When he had cleared his well-filled dinner plate he went round to all the other plates and scooped the leftovers onto his own.

We spent that night together in a shippen and I was far too weary to bother in the slightest, not caring if Old Nick himself had been my nocturnal companion. In the morning a youth came to rouse us. Frank scarpered out of the hay and went off across the fields, not bothering to enquire if he would be required for further work. I was glad to see him leave so I offered my services for the day and the lad came back to tell me I could stay. He picked something up from where Frank had been lying. "This your parcel?" he asked. I shook my head. It was a newspaper bundle and when he opened it a pile of one pound notes fell to the floor. Later, when handed to the farmer in the kitchen, there were found to be exactly one hundred.

"Well bugger me," said the farmer. "He's better of nor I am."

Nevertheless, he sent the lad off after Frank who was still visible climbing the Fell side. When the lad returned he told us that Frank had scowled at him and muttered, 'give me that you!" and then proceeded to count each note slowly and deliberately before going on his way without even a word of thanks to the sweating lad who had chased him up the Fell.

Several years later I read in a National paper that a well-known Lunesdale tramp had been found dead in a barn in Yorkshire. I knew from the description that it was Frank the tramp. The story was headline news for on his body was found over a thousand pounds in notes!

The story was further enlarged upon by a village policeman whom I had always found to be friendly to roadsters provided they didn't indulge in downright begging. Then the police felt compelled to move us on and it was only in the extreme circumstances that they ran us in for begging and vagrancy. This particular policeman began to speak about Frank. He told me that a solicitor had unearthed the facts of his former life. His two brothers were still in business in a town which he did not name. 'Up Newcastle way' he said evasively when I tried to probe. Frank had been the black sheep of the family and had blotted the family copybook with indelible ink with his philandering ways. The brothers, in an effort to preserve the good name of the family, had paid him out of the business and Frank had taken to the road to escape the attentions of the husbands of his former lovers.

There were often some fascinating stories buried deep in the ragged clothes of the old grey tramp. Frank had spoiled many a good mark for his fellow roadsters and not a man or woman amongst us was sorry to hear of his death.

From Kirkby the countryside takes on a new characteristic going Northwards. I always took the hard route to Kendal because I found it worthwhile and far less frequented by fellow roadsters than the main road. I took the Sedbergh (pronounced Sedber) road but soon left it to cut across country through the village of Casterton. I have never visited Sedbergh because I was told that, second to Shap, it had the worst tramp-ward in Britain. You would have thought that these more inaccessible places would have had more comfortable wards, but they were usually worse for the governors knew that men who had no money for a doss had no option but to sleep rough under the stars.

This is no reason not to visit a town but a tramp's reasons for travelling were much different to the tourists. I am told that Sedbergh is a beautiful town and as it is but a few miles beyond the patch I travelled I do not doubt it. For this is magnificent country — a rolling terrain of Fells, tumbling becks, majestic hills and green grassy hollows. Like Bowland and Lunesdale, it is great sheep country and helped to bring prosperity to the wool town of Kendal. The road I followed is a tortuous one even now, but what I suffered at one end, namely feet, I made up for at the other end. For the eyes are regaled by some quite breath-taking scenes.

As I have already said, tramps don't as a rule climb mountains, but on one occasion I struggled to see the tops of Gregareth and was rewarded by stupendous views to compensate for the aching muscles and the time lost in making money. For I had to live solely for the day; only on the rare, fortunate occasion did I have money left over for the morrow. To the east I saw the Valley of the Vikings, Kingsdale, an area rich in Viking folk-lore and legends kept alive by the names of places such as Yordas Cave and Braida Garth. I could see lovely Ingleborough and Penny Ghent Mountain, wild and free and capped with snow; the quiet dignity of rolling moorland, the moorlands of the Pennine Range, and north-west my eyes took in the Peaks of the Lake District — Langdale, great Gable and Coniston, whilst south were softer valley areas with trees and streams. Each view represented a mood of man — fierceness, arrogance, dignity and tenderness. I have never been sorry when I have climbed a mountain.

And through it the lovely Lune winds its way to the sea, whilst seemingly endless dry stone walls, skilfully built by the Fell farmers, divide the scene into a patchwork of beauty one would have to travel hundreds of miles to equal.

I can never think of the Lune without tasting again the glorious grilled salmon I have taken from its waters. Which naturally, leads me on to the noble art of poaching! Many the fish I have extracted from the riparian landlords. But the tastiest of all belonged to Lord and Lady Henry Cavendish Bentink. This aristocratic couple were well revered in Kirkby and district for they provided a lot of work, but I am sure that they were not aware that when they were dining on salmon caught in the Lune a scruffy tramp was also doing the same in some wood or under a bridge. I have never considered that poaching is stealing. Many country folk had to poach in order to live. I knew many families who had been brought up on the proceeds of skilful poaching. I also knew of prominent men who indulged in it for the thrill and adventure. But to me it was stictly business, and like all business men I had to have my customers. The source of my supply was never discussed, naturally, and I was aware that one of my customers was the wife of a well-known judge. So I can truthfully say that tramp and judge have dined off the same fish.

I have used nearly all the known poaching methods, all gleaned from careful listening to expert poachers in the doss-houses and men I have met along the road and river banks, and put into practise in all kinds of weather. I have gone out 'lamping' at night as a helper to a local poacher, acting as watch-dog and hauler-in. The lamp is strapped to the poacher's waist. The light mesmerises the salmon. Quick as a flash the four-pronged barbed fork is thrust into the fish. This is mounted on the end of a pole to which is tied a good length of rope. The weapon is known as a reester and was made by blacksmiths for the poachers. Many blacksmiths had little sidelines not known to the general public or the police.

My favourite method of poaching was the snare; it is less cumbersome and does not make a mess of the fish like the reester. But I tried for many weary hours before mastering the art. My first fish was a sea trout taken from a beck. These becks often hold lovely fish which come up to spawn. The poacher lies on a rock or on the bank, having spotted the rear end of a fish protruding from its lie beneath a sheltering rock or the overhang of the bank. The snare works in the same way as the trout-tickler's fingers. The loop of the snare tickles the fish which will remain motionless. Gradually, and with great care, the loop is worked along the body and sufficiently far enough along it is suddenly snatched and yet another fish leaves the water. I have caught a salmon in the morning and a rabbit in the afternoon on the same snare.

Both these methods are more enjoyable than night lining which is a messy business and often the worms are harder to catch than the fish. Disposing of the fish had to be done quickly and I always carried a knife with which to cut it up into portions. Early morning milkmen and postmen were used by poachers for carrying fish into a village. They were beyond suspicion. Likewise, the tramp, and I was never stopped by the police or a bailiff to have my sack searched. For although he was welcomed by most country folk there was something slightly fearful about him which acted as protection.

During the bad depression times men would come from inland towns to poach. Water bailiffs were kept fully employed and many poachers were caught. Some were sent to prison. Although I didn't know it at the time, one of the local poachers, who considered that his stretch of river was sacred to him alone, was becoming very annoyed by these activities. The water bailiffs were over-active, making life quite unbearable for him. One day I called at a house and sold a nice 'cut' of salmon to a lady. As it was a large fish I had several pieces to sell, so I asked her if she knew of anyone else who would be interested. This was clandestine business and so the less said the better. She simply told me to try the old chap at the cottage down the lane. "He knows about such things," she said as she paid me quickly and closed the door. The 'old chap,' who was hardly fifty, was digging in the garden. I approached him and told him that I thought he might know of someone who would like a nice steak of fresh salmon, or maybe he would be partial to one himself. He eyed me angrily, or so I thought. I should have acted on impulse and departed quickly, but when he suddenly became quite friendly I was lulled into thinking he could oblige me.

"Aye, I know a chap that'll have a piece all right," he said and pointed to a house along the lane. "Knock on the door and tell him what you've got. He'll be very interested."

I thanked him and set off for the cottage he had indicated. It had a wide stone wall and on the gate pillar I saw the sign ⓟ. An experienced roadster by this time, I knew my tramp signs and that this one was a warning left by another tramp who had obviously received a very hostile reception.

Knowing that the sign meant "Will send for police" I was immediately on my guard, crossed the road and sat on the river bridge where a young lad was rolling 'stonies' on the flat stone of the bridge wall. "Who lives in the house yonder?" I asked him.

"Water bailiff Mr – – – mister." Once more the cabalistic sign language of the road had saved me. I took a scrap of paper from my sack and wrote the guardian of the river a little note which read:

If you want to catch a poacher red-handed go to Rose Cottage and you'll find a piece of freshly caught salmon on the kitchen table. I watched him take it in the house.

I folded the paper. "Do you want to earn a penny, lad?" I asked the boy.

His eyes sparkled. "Thanks mister," he said.

I gave him the note. "Count up to fifty slowly then go over and knock on the door, then hand the note to the bailiff."

"Reet, mister. I seed him go in not long ago for his dinner."

I walked back up the lane towards the cottage. The local poacher (I have since found out that this was who he was) was still digging in the garden. I crossed a wall into a field and so avoided catching his eye. The back door of his cottage was conveniently open so I was able to enter and place the remains of the fish on a table. Then, clambering part way up the Fell side, I had a good view of the cottage and the lane. The lad was still rolling 'stonies' on the bridge and along the lane a man was riding a bike furiously. Flinging it from him at the cottage gate, he stormed into the garden with all the outraged authority one would expect from a bailiff determined to see justice done. I had lost a nice piece of highly profitable fish, but I had the satisfaction of knowing that the local coppers' nark, and the local poacher to boot, had been paid back in his own coin. I later heard that this man had reported several other people for 'poaching' on *his* preserves.

The battle between poacher and bailiff and gamekeeper

was a constant one and I witnessed many a fight as I lay in hiding in a wood. After one such fight two poachers tied a gamekeeper to a gate then after lifting it from its hinges flung it so that he lay face down on a ploughed field. The tramp was always on the side it paid him to be on, and this time I soon went to the help of the gamekeeper, but not before I had given him a good ten minutes of the discomfort to make his rescue all the sweeter. I received a shilling and a three-course lunch in return. Another time I witnessed a far more barbaric trick. The keeper had surprised three men poaching pheasants on a Lunesdale preserve. One of them kicked up soil into his face and relieved him of his gun, then they carried him across to land which was riddled with rabbit holes and, first of all spreading his arms wide, they thrust his head face downward into a burrow. Next, they tied his wrists with rope which they attached to stakes of wood driven into the ground, a fiendishly bizarre form of crucifixion. Living off the land and the people, like I did, I saw many cruelties but this was the most barbaric of all and, again, I was well rewarded for my rescue.

In all my years poaching I was never caught, but this I attribute mainly to my nomadic existence for, not having any roots, I had no friends except for the other wanderers I met. I was a loner with no accomplices to turn informer for a reward. Mostly I would work by night, walking by the river sides by day, taking mental notes of good lies and learning the most important lesson of all — the movements of the bailiff.

Chesterton said that it was the rolling English drunk who made the rolling English road. If this is so then the man who made the road I took to Kendal must have been a devoted disciple of Bacchus. But despite its corkscrew meanderings, a rolling English tramp never failed to arrive in the Quaker town of Kendal in the early hours of the morning, the better to transact a hugger-mugger deal concerned with a nice cut of Lune salmon illicitly caught by moonlight.

8

ON THE WAY TO THE LAKES

Kendal is a large country town set at an important junction from many points of the compass, a town which in my tramping days was on the main highway between England and Scotland; then, when one considers it is the gateway to the Lakes, there can be no doubting its tremendous capacity for business of all kinds. Nowadays there is no need to go through the town and the terrible ordeal of Shap (more of this later) is just another chapter in the story of transport history.

Kendal was a great place for tramps — a swarming hive for all kinds of travellers. On a market day you would have sworn that half the nomadic population of Britain was gathered there; horse-dealers, sheep-dealers, quack medicine men, market salesmen of every hue from the honest to the downright crooked; pedlars, quacker tale-pitchers (preachers), beggars, buskers, mug fakers (photographers), dolly mops (prostitutes) and of course that 'son of rest' — the tramp. Add gipsies, Scottish tinkers, Irish navvies and harvest-time workers and you had as varied an itinerant cocktail as you would meet in any town in the country. It follows that Kendal had many lodging houses of various denominations, with one part of the town — now levelled to the ground to make way for road development — notorious for its tramp-dens. And what rough places some of them were, particularly the one we roadsters called 'Hairy Mary's'. The police were hardly ever away for she harboured all kinds of criminals. It was a house I avoided if at all possible even though cheap. She let the lodgers sleep in the kitchen if they hadn't got the kip money, and as well as turning a blind eye to all illicit dealings she encouraged the street women to use the house for their business. It was the original den of iniquity and I knew many hardened tramps who considered they were plumbing the depths if they were forced to stay at 'Hairy Mary's'. She kept two pet rats as big as small cats and it wasn't unusual to find one lying on the sofa when you awoke in the morning, or even nestling at the foot of the bed like a pet poodle. The sight of a rat seldom worried the tramp. It was here I saw Wigan Will fight Penrith Abe. Both were noted bruisers who had conducted a vendetta against each other for many years. Drum-up was in progress and it mattered not who was at the stove when either entered. You simply gave way unless you wanted a black eye, for both would hit you first and speak after. On the evening in question they were at the stove together, a smouldering silence, a chance meeting and only one word needed to represent the spark to set off the fuse of violence. An absent-minded tramp named Speccy Foreshaw stuck his fork into Wigan Will's pan and speared a piece of bacon. Will immediately flew at Speccy, hitting him across the face with the back of his hand. Now Abe had travelled that day with Speccy and willingly took up the fight on his behalf. The rest of us removed ourselves as far from the battle area as possible. Drum-up was brought to an abrupt end as Abe swept the pans from the stove in the direction of Will, then both met in a clinch, biting, banging heads until they cast each other aside like great apes. For a full half hour that kitchen became the slogging pitch for an old-time fist fight. Blood ran on the floor and lay in pools on the tables. And yet, for all its ferocity, there was never a dirty action in the fisticuffs until Wigan Will finished it by kicking Penrith Abe in the groin with a steel-toed clog. I witnessed fights in those days that men would have paid a guinea for a ring-side seat had they been in a Boxing Hall.

Mary had her own doctor, a shady character who carried out back-street abortions at five pounds a time. He was a clever surgeon and patched both men up with the aid of buckets of hot water and carbolic and a neat stitching job with suture and needle. After it was over and with three or four pints of tea inside them, they shook hands and went to a pub for a drink. We assumed that the vendetta was now at an end, but the next day was to produce a startling anti-climax to the supposed reconciliation.

In the way of tramps, we had planned our routes for the next day over supper drum-up and both the gladiators were present, seemingly friendly and co-operative. I was going North to Shap after a spell in the market lumping potato sacks for a smallholder I knew, while Wigan Will was going to Windermere, as also was Penrith Abe. Two men on the one road was quite enough and even if anyone else had thoughts of travelling the Windermere road they soon relinquished them when they knew these men would be on it. Come the morning the toss of a coin decided which of them should take to the road first. Abe had a double-headed penny unknown to Will and, naturally enough, shouted 'heads' when I spun it for them. I had spotted the trickery but was too fond of my skin to bring it to the notice of Will, for I quite often met Abe along the road. So Abe, having won the toss, started out half-an-hour in front of Will, the advantage being that the first tramp got the best of the pickings. After this the story is purely hearsay but true enough. Will, following in the wake of Abe, came across a farmhouse four miles out of Kendal. On the gate was the mark ⊗ signifying 'very hospitable'. The same mark was on another gate and as Will progressed to the house he saw it yet again. Inside the farmyard a massive Alsation flung itself from an overhead barn doorway and savaged the intruding tramp. Will spent six weeks in Kendal Infirmary and was fortunate to come out alive. He died in a Yorkshire Workhouse a year later, never having fully recovered from his wounds. Of course he had fallen for an old tramp trick, not a common one but a means of revenge which could be quite terrible.

*   *   *   *

Kendal is steeped in history. Riddled with winding alleys, nooks and crannies, its long main street housing over a hundred gateways to the 'yards' spaced at near intervals along both sides of the street. These 'yards' are really roads or narrow streets containing houses. Wool was stored in them and they could be closed at both ends, the prime concern being the preservation of the lives of the residents from invaders. It is, too, a town which hangs grimly on to its past, but in the days between the two wars little effort had been made to alter its ancient face. It reeked of antiquity, the sort of place where one would like to have taken a blindfolded tourist and, upon releasing the fold, said, "Now this is England." for it was the very essence of the England pictured and described in geographical and tourist books. Along the main street from the Parish church by the Kent bank, going northward, stood dozens of antique shops whose murky windows sported all manner of objects d'art and bric-a-brac; whilst pots, pans, porcelain and pewter blended together in cobwebbed confusion with violin bows and candlesticks fraternising in brass buckets. But to me the greatest attraction of the town were the cook-shops with their appetising aromas, tantalisingly out of reach to the majority of wanderers. The regular caller knew his haunts and I became familiar with those butchers who were good for two pennyworth of meat which was considered too poor in quality to sell — dog's meat — but good enough for a tramp to grill on the stove or fry up with a pennyworth of scrap vegetables from a greengrocer. Some butchers and greengrocers were kindly and always kept a little under the counter for the regular tramp, often for no charge. But Kendal and the district around it for many miles was poor hunting ground for the tramp begging for money, for this was, and still is to some degree, Quaker territory. Not that the sect were antagonistic to tramps; on the contrary, they were often hospitable and kind for their Faith had been built upon hardship and oppression and they looked with charity on those who were genuinely down on their luck. But they waged continual war against the demon drink, and the title 'tramp' was synonymous with this 'evil'. I once went up to a Quaker's door, my breath smelling of a single glass of beer I had drunk and for my sins was chased down the path by a black-frocked fellow who could have passed for a cohort of Death himself. So, with these people it was kindness often in the form of old clothing or tea and bread, but never money for they knew that money could purchase the 'strong waters', as all forms of alcohol were known to the abstemious classes. But the savoir-faire of the professional tramp would have hoodwinked St. Peter into opening those Pearly Gates.

Deception soon became an integral part of my character and I regularly lived a lie; a young man can start out in life with pure purpose of honest endeavour but when living depends upon a choice between the high, lofty principles of theoretical piety and the practical down-to-earth necessity of twisting truth to fill an empty belly, then he is put to a test in which weight of conscience can be cast aside like a pebble by sheer force of temptation. I 'told the tale' to live, pretended and played upon the sympathy of those who had a roof over their heads. Times have not changed too much, the genuine tramp has been replaced by the government sponsored sponger, the man who draws his Social Security and is given his doss-money, who turns the larger cities and towns into dosser-colonies. The 'tramp' has lost his image. Today his counterpart is better dressed but he has lost his character. He is no longer a romantic figure and with this loss of image has gone his attraction to the respectable side of society. For many folk secretly envied the old time roadsters, but they are now more inclined to look with disdain on the modern brood, no matter how genuine some of them are. The road is no longer the master of the tramp. He has relinquished it and is now a town dweller — down-and-out, wino, call him what you will. But there is still a marked similarity between them in as much that a man can improve his condition by his ability to tell the tale. In my day particularly, long before State sponsorship of vagrants, this art determined whether a man barely existed or lived in relative comfort.

I found a natural adaptability to deception, a latent badness in my character maybe, the heart-tugging of my overtures were a sure means of getting me what I wanted. Or, maybe, I was a born actor never given the chance of a legitimate stage; my stage was the door-step and my lines would vary on the spur of the moment, no prompter needed to nudge the memory. As a Catholic orphan boy I was excellent and would soon have the women crying and how I would sing the praises of the Pope for a mugful of tea and a pork pie. I once stole a Catholic Bible from another tramp. He had stolen it, too, and I don't doubt that it had been through the hands of several tramps in the same way. Besides, he had stolen a jacket of mine and I was simply setting the score to rights; and that grubby, well-thumbed book was a boon. What I liked about Catholics was the fact that they advertised their religion by holy pictures and all manner of religious objects, so a man knew he could bring out his papal patter safely. The best method, of course, would have been to have had the prayer books appropriate for the beliefs of all religions, but my finances could never run to such props. On one trip along the road to Windermere I chanced on a Catholic homestead, the family were on their knees saying the rosary. I was brought into the house for once and given a glass of milk, warm from the cow. I placed my bible on the table and after drinking the milk buried my face in my hands and knelt down on the stone kitchen floor. When the prayers were over the wife picked up the book. "Look, a Bible, Martin," she said to her husband, "and him on the road, poor fellow. Now isn't it privileged we are to be able to let him share a meal?"

"But I haven't had a meal — yet," I pointed out, for I had long since lost the shyness of early days.

"But you soon will have — yes, you will indeed. It's a wonderful thing to see a young chap on the road and him still clinging to his Bible. That's real Faith."

"It was my mother's. She was Irish, too." This pleased the woman and she turned to her husband.

"Sure, he recognised the accent, Martin, and me over here this forty years — oh! God bless you, lad, for a true son of your mother."

The Thespian in me sprang at the prompt. "She's dead, God rest her soul. Consumption, the house was sold over my head and I'm out of work."

Now the Irish love a sad story as much as they love a sad song and I laid it on thick and heavy, emphasising the hardships I had endured and stringing such a litany of hard luck together that I wonder now how anyone swallowed it. I threw in a couple of unhappy love affairs (the purest kind of course) and a cruel boss or two for good measure and when I heard the heart-warming sob of sympathy I knew it was enough. My next task was to deliver thanks and benedictions upon the head of the benefactor. It went well.

"God love you for a steadfast Catholic — you see, God has looked after you despite it all. You've been rocked and blown on the sea of life but you are still afloat — God love you for a son of your poor mother — rest her soul — it's the wee Bible that's done it — God protect you. That little Book will bring you comfort and rewards, God knows it will."

In this case it was a great feed of boiled bacon and cabbage and a good clean mattress in the loft with a breakfast on the morrow to set me on my way and sustain me until the evening time. Yes, that little book was well worth pinching. I have prayed with Quakers, joined in a bawdy song about the Pope with a gang of Orangemen out on the razzle, and hallelujahed with the best of them in a tin Mission hut because I knew there was a plate of corned beef and pickles at the end of it. And I still had the affrontery to risk God's justful wrath by walking out each day.

I had acquired the worst tramp habits. If I had been offered permanent work I would have rejected it, for tramping was now my life. After all, I had known little of conventional life and after several years living in the nomadic way I was in love with the freedom. Seeing poverty on every mean street corner of every mean town I passed through only made me aware that I was better off than those young lads and men loafing hopelessly on the streets and towns that had become the breeding grounds of despair and disenchantment. I even grew to despise these 'young mugs'. My early days on the circuit had seen me almost cringing in shame at the speech of the old-hand tramps who thought all work-seeking men fools, yet they, too, might have started out on the road seeking work but lack of employment knocks the gumption out of a man, reduces him to a beggar in spirit, kills pride and, if sustained, breeds in him the chronic resentment of the vagabond.

The genuine tramp, which I became, constituted a smaller proportion of the whole vagrant population than is generally supposed; he was the type of incurable nomad whom novelists idealise as the freedom-seeker supreme, the man who had turned his back on society, left the tramlines of life for the unshackled *carte-blanche* of travel and modus operandi; the hater of rules and regulations who, in turning his back on society, had willingly accepted the hardships and the rough side of the coin of a life where one was classless – a nobody – and yet I found that, along with this state of nonentity, there existed a sort of limbo of spirit to which no other beings were admitted. I was an isolationist, an island, having a communion with a nature normal man did not know existed; the birds and animals became my friends and companions, the flowers and trees my boon comrades. I delighted in their moods, but when all is said and done, the soul of the tramp laid bare, it was the road itself that was the prime reason for my tramping. The power of the call of the road, Man's insatiable appetite for adventure, his inborn desire to see the view around the next corner; frustrated desires in most men, beaten out of them by the accepted code of respectability which does not condone the eccentric in its ordered scheme of things, but in the tramp it took root and thrived until it became a plant so strong that no amount of pruning or directing could alter the course of its meanderings – the road called and the tramp followed. He loved the road, loved the life and would not, could not, change.

I readily own up now to having been a petty criminal, a simple matter of progression from tale-spinning to petty felony. In Ambleside I was desperate for money, the hallway of a hotel was unoccupied. Espying a carpet of a handy size for carrying, I rolled it up in the twinkling of an eye and walked out with it underneath my arm, not a soul taking any notice. A fence was lodging at the doss-house and he handed me a ten shilling note for the carpet, unknown to the proprietors who, in fairness to them, did not condone such business.

"Pity you've not got the rest," said the fence.

So back I went and removed the underfelt in the same nonchalant way. For this I received a two shilling piece.

And writing of two shilling pieces reminds me of the

collection plate trick I thought up whilst on my travels. Its first testing place was a protestant church on the Windermere road. Now, for a tramp to present himself in church for a Sunday service was rather unusual, but this I did, and here it might better help the Reader to appreciate the scene if I describe my appearance at this point of my vagabondage: Thirty-five was my age but I could easily have passed for fifty; all roadsters looked older than they were. For I had the hair and beard long and bushy needed to help the illusion along, face tanned by many years of sunlight and winds, body spare but fit with my six foot frame, for the most part, covered by a grubby macintosh held together round the waist by a piece of rope, my trousers were someone's cast-offs and my boots plainly showing that I was not short of ventilation. Such was the figure I cut on that Sabbath morning, a disturbing contrast to the rest of the congregation, even the farm labourers and their families, seated in the back pews, who sported clothes obviously stored away after every Sunday so that they would do service for many more Sundays to come. The squirarchy and the lesser ranks of gentility were conspicuous by their degrees of separation in the pews and I wondered if these folk really believed that a similar system existed in Heaven where Philpotts, the banker, would have a better seat than Meredith, the insurance agent, and so on with the shopkeepers and the trades folk lucky to get a seat at all. I really think that they did. The stupidity and snobbery of middle-class England in the Thirties was never more apparent than when it went to church.

Pompous sidesmen stared at the interloper who had dared to go to church and as I faced the varying degrees of disgust upon the faces of the congregation, I fought back the desire to flee the place and stared back. My pew remained singularly uncluttered — from other humans I mean. On one side of me was my sack of belongings, whilst a clutter of receptacles, i.e. kettle, cooking pot and an old tin helmet, were strung together and lay on the bench on my other side. There was no doubting a tramp had come to pray — or maybe I should spell the word with an 'e' instead of an 'a'. My occupation of so much room, and the disinclination of other Christians to join me, threw the normal seating structure into some confusion. I had caused a social upheaval, causing a schoolteacher to share his pew with a shopkeeper. The system in most churches was similar to the state of affairs in cricket where the Gentlemen didn't mix with the Professionals even though they played for the same team. A flat cap and clogs in the best stand at Lords couldn't have caused any more consternation than my arrival in that church. Outraged sidesmen fumed inwardly.

My presence well and truly noticed by all, including the vicar, the service began and when the sidesman made it perfectly obvious that he didn't consider that thrusting his long-handled box in my direction would be beneficial to the church funds, I called him back. My hand was outstretched, the man was nervous, considering, from his facial expression, that extraction of coinage was more likely than subscription. The box loomed. I twiddled. To twiddle, dip the fingers into the coins and 'twiddle'. No man can rightly say you haven't put a coin on the plate, if you do it correctly. Black eyebrows arched, suspicion in brown eyes beneath them shone as bright and clear as the impression gleaned that the vicar had focused his sermon on the evils of over-indulgence upon me; yet there was incredulity in them, too, mixed with that look all pompous men have when someone has defied them.

Not one person as much as nodded at me as they made their way out, but I didn't care for my business was with the vicar. He was disrobing as I was reluctantly let into the vestry by the disapproving church-warden.

"It's that tramp, vicar," he hissed through his teeth in the manner of a man plagued by the wretches.

"Come in — come in," sang the cleric, showing a desire to compensate for the lack of Christian welcome by his congregation.

"I wouldn't have bothered you, vicar — only — well — being poor, like —"

"He's a beggar, sir," crowed the little tin god of the church.

"Leave him be, Mr Hopkins — carry on," said the vicar, turning to me.

"I was at the service, sir — well — I mean, as I said, sir — I haven't much, me being on the pad — well, I made a mistake, see, when I put money in the box. I mean . . ."

"You gave to the collection?" The vicar was impressed, uplifted. The church-warden's eyes were gimlets of disbelief.

"Well, I like to — but — well, not being well fixed I ain't got much to spare . . ." Wringing my hands, I purred — doing my Uriah Heap act for all I was worth.

"One wouldn't expect a — a man of your — er — limited means to give a lot." I had the poor chap embarrassed.

"Well, I put a two shilling piece on instead of a penny." I exposed a penny in the palm of my hand. "And it's all I've got in the world, vicar."

The vicar ignored the church-warden's open-mouthed look and handed me a florin from the box. I offered him the penny in return. He refused it saying, "Keep the coin, my son. Get yourself some food. The spirit is willing, go on your way rejoicing like the lost sheep who returned to the fold."

'Aye, but it's you who's been fleeced, mate' was the message in the church-warden's eyes.

And so, I did as his reverence said, fingering the coin bright and beautiful. A week later I repeated the trick twice, in different churches in Penrith, but this time I abandoned the twiddling routine and actually placed a penny on the plate just in case my sleight-of-hand was spotted. Cast your bread upon the waters said the Good Book, and I was on a jolly good profit.

The following weekend saw me in Barrow, seeking the company of seamen in the dockside pubs. Matelots were always open-handed, particularly when in drink, which was nearly all the time while on shore leave, and a Canadian deckhand found the adventures of an English 'hobo' to be well worth paying for in the form of beer and a two shilling piece gratuity. The Sabbath saw me at Mass in a Catholic church, a hangover clouding my thought process, and the florin nestling comfortably with two pennies in my coat pocket. Beware of a befuddled brain you who try to cheat the Lord! If there was a tract on the subject, that's what it would say. I placed my coin on the plate and then a cold sweat engulfed me. I fumbled furiously in my pocket. Two pennies were in my fingers. I had put the florin on the plate.

The fat parish priest was remonstrating with an altar boy as I stood at the open door of the sacristy.

"And what d'ye want?" asked the P.P.

"I put a two shilling piece on the plate, Father — instead of a penny. I've only twopence left, Father — it was a mistake, Father — honest."

"Honest!" He uttered a massive belly laugh. "Honest! You, honest — God forgive you. I was expectin' yourself and here ye are — get away wich ye or I'll have the polis on ye. Didn't Mister Brown, the verger in Penrith, 'phone me to warn me there was a rapscallion of a rogue going round the churches —"

"But I *did* put silver on the plate this time — ask the collector, Father — please —" My pleading was in vain.

Opening the door, he said. "On your way, Riley. The Lord loves a trier."

The early Thirties was a time of great recruitment to the tramp army. Two young mugs turned up at Kendal padding-ken one night at drum-up. The most of us were smoking a supper pipe or attending to our chores, such as washing shirts or boiling trousers on the range. Some nights the doss-house kitchen would resemble a laundry. The newcomers were decrepit even by vagrant standards, the seats out of their trousers and them the colour of a sweep's face, while extreme hunger bit into every line of their faces; and yet there was pride, too, that stupid pride which defies logic and tumbles the harder for the tragedy of its fall. They were both honest to goodness hard-working chaps, given a chance, lads who would have given value for money to any boss. Yet they were jobless, products of the national slump — young mugs to us tramps who looked on all who worked for a living as fools. And yet I had been like these men once. I, too, had had pride, stubborn pride. The one with ginger hair made no secret, by the expression on his face, that he strongly resented lodging with tramps. There was a military look about him, a presence obvious even when sitting in a tramps' doss-den looking decidedly worse off than the tramps. His companion was dreadfully pale and looked to be on the verge of collapse. Neither appeared to have any food.

"Cuppa tea, lads?" sang out Ginger Cush whose forte was

wringing chickens' necks.

"No thanks," snapped the dominant one of the duo. The pale one gulped and whispered something into the other one's ear. His friend's refusal of the tea was a bitter disappointment. "We'll not take charity from a lot of tramps," hissed the other, not at all quietly.

"You might turn your noses up at us tramps, lads, but who's the mugs, us or you?" A huge black-maned beggar by the name of Scutchy towered above them. "You wanna brew, lad, don't you?" He addressed the question to the pale, lank one. The answer was a quiet nod. Ginger Cush placed a mug in front of him. Whether it was the size of Scutchy or the sight of the tea, but the other man accepted a cup. Both cups were drained and refilled.

"Now then, lads," Scutchy addressed us all, "these two lads could do with a meal. Now come on get rooting. You know the rule - no grub to be taken out of the kip house."

We all began to search. The rule he alluded to was not a hard and fast ritual, but a commonsense fact of road lore. We were a practical tribe in many ways. Tramps were not philanthropists with poorer members of the fraternity but abhorred waste and it was considered wasteful to take away food from the lodging house. Besides, most tramps' clothing was verminous, food did not gain in flavour by being kept so any leftovers were shared out, maybe bartered for tea, or other useful commodities. And so Frank and James, as our two 'young mugs' were named, were provided with a good wholesome meal apiece by the joint efforts of the assembly and, once returned to something resembling normality, they began to talk.

They were Wiganers, both ex-soldiers, the dominant redhead an officer, both had been made redundant. Frank, the ex-officer, told a story closely following my own experience; though an older man than I was when seeking work. Gradually he sank to the casual ward circuit and teamed up with James, a coalminer, offering their services unsuccessfully to any who cared to listen. Both despised their way of life. Hearing that hop-pickers were needed in Kent they tramped hopefully to the hop fields. All they found were roadsides lined with men, women and children, whole families in some cases, living and sleeping close to the fields in the hope of a few hours work. They got none and were forced to spend night after night in spikes, fulfilling the mandate laid down by the Workhouse Unions. Each morning wood-chopping or stone-breaking undertaken in return for meagre rations of bread and margarine, weak porridge and tea, never both.

But though they were ashamed to go to casual wards, they were horrified to think that they would perhaps spend a night in a doss-house. Now the logic of this was topsy-turvy because a lodging-house meant they had some money, however little, and gave them independence. They were not State prisoners, as in the spike, but it was the dread of whom they would meet in the doss-house; this was the abyss, the Gehenna, the habitation of fallen angels. And yet here they were spending the money they had made by scrambling for coal on slag heaps; here they were being fed by a gang of men whose very title had, only minutes earlier, been an affront to their sense of dignity; here they were the clay tramps are made from.

The ex-officer apologised in his own way, "I'm sorry, men. Only we aren't used to hand-outs, James and I. More kicks than ha'pence as they say."

Then Scutchy began a lecture which condemned the British Government system, especially the rich, the cotton magnates, shipping owners, colliery owners and all bloated plutocrats, for the rich were the avowed enemies of all tramps in those days — in fact, of all who were *not* rich — and I could see the process of change, metamorphosis occurring already in the characters of two men; yet Scutchy was right, they owed it to themselves to find a means of livelihood, these apprentices to the road where a man lived on his wits and turned survival into a trade, yet I knew that once upon that road they could not return, they would not, nor want to. Once a tramp always a tramp except in very rare circumstances.

And so Frank and James began their apprenticeship upon the stretch from Kendal to Windermere; and what memories I have of this stretch which leads to the lovely regions known as Lakeland. Both roamed the roads for many years, simply two examples of recruitment to an ever moving, useless army of men who paraded up and down, across and around the country in a never ceasing stream of humanity producing no end product either to themselves or to the country.

This was a good road for 'calls'. I was welcome at most houses, always having something to sell; not alone of my advantages was the news I carried. Many people didn't take newspapers then and the wireless was only a new-fangled gadget, and so the news carrier was always welcome. I had a retentive memory and would make a point of listening to any news I heard in Kendal, particularly making sure to collect newspapers from bins, and perhaps a visit to the Reading-room of the Library. The medieval tramp-travellers carried news — it was tradition — and I was following in the time-worn footsteps of the journeymen and the pedlars; these latter men were still to be seen on the roads, but rarely. They were not tramps, but men who carried a stock in a bag slung over their shoulders — travelling scotchmen was their nickname — the forerunners of the present-day travelling shops. The pedlar sold all manner of small goods and his visits were held in great favour by the householders, particularly the ladies. These packmen were often great storytellers, too, and usually slept in barns or along the roadsides beneath hedges in the summer. Having such valuable cargoes, they had more sense than to sleep in doss-houses. With a stock of laces and pins and needles I was following in the footsteps of these characters, but whereas the pedlar was a business man, however humble, I was just a tramp and my position was always impressed upon me by people's reluctance to let me past the front doorstep. Among the travelling fraternity the tramp was known as a mumper. He was the lowest — the gipsies, knife-grinders, pedlars and the rest were higher up the scale and would have been deeply insulted to have been branded as tramps. But be that as it may I lived well in the Lake District.

9

THE LAKES

I always maintain that the true Lakeland scenery begins at Windermere. And what is there left to say about the Lakes that has not been said already hundreds of times? I travelled the area for many years, seeing its myriad facets of mood-colour and mirrored beauty of wild water continually unveiling, and yet on each visit I discovered new beauty, fresh delights; the compelling majesty of mountain lakes and tarns. I have felt in perfect communion with the remotest regions; a soul-affinity with the mountains, where man is away from all the cares and troubles of life; free as a goat above the lake so dark and deep, the surrounding mountains towering over it like great silent sentinels — guards set by Time itself to ensure that some dread secret is kept intact. I have felt the solemnity, the strange almost weird silence of the place as I have ascended the boulder-strewn slopes, where feeder streams sweep in their bubbling waters from the heights above. There is a whispering in the brake; that soughing music of high lonely places, a soulful dirge and yet it is not an unhappy sound, but an integral part of the Lake District entering the soul; yet the mind cannot locate it or the ear define it. I have heard of mountain men speak of such whisperings that are not real sounds but live chords struck aeons ago in the misty past of an early Christianity, voices crying in the heather, in the bracken, rising from bogland and lakeside; no man can say what the sound is but all men can hear it. It is woven into the fabric of a man's soul. But the cynic does not let it enter into his being, trying to dismiss it; the dreamer stops, listens and so did the tramp, for he was akin to the nature of the sound having returned to a nature most men had disregarded, and so he understood. He saw vague figures flitting through the cobwebs of time; he was back in those violent days of Norman rule when the valleys and mountains were the camping grounds for the French soldiers. But these troops were not at peace amongst such unfamiliar terrain, longing for the plains of their native Normandy. Their spirits were slowly demoralized; morale crushed, they feared the winds that tore around the crags, whistling through the valleys like mad demons. To them this was an evil land of enchantment where the Powers of Darkness played dreadful tricks and where there were marshes, notorious for swallowing up their horses daily; tales were told and spread like forest fire amongst the troops that demons and giants roamed the Fells and made their homes in mountain caves. Pack-mules disappeared mysteriously in this land of mists and rain. Until, finally, the conquering Norman troops were crushed in spirit and deserted. Perhaps they were soulless creatures, perhaps they were just frightened by the primaeval mystery of the place. It still exists. I have felt it; those soul-sounds are the fluid essence of its very being. And yet I knew a deep tranquility whenever I was there. My pulse never failed to be stirred, I was aware of a strange feeling of privilege — I cannot describe it, I simply call it the Magic of the Lake District.

* * * *

The song-writer W.S. Gilbert touched on many subjects in his bizarre compositions, but one I liked to sing to myself whilst trudging the lanes was a song which summed up the character of many tramps. Rogues of varying sorts many of us were but the country men were lovers of Nature:

When a felon's not engaged in his employment,
Or maturing his felonious little plan,
His capacity for innocent enjoyment
Is just as great as any honest man . . .

When the enterprising burglar's not a-burglaring.
When the cut-throat isn't occupied in crime,

He likes to hear the little brook a-gurgling,
And listen to the merry village chimes . . .

I was fortunate, for how could any normal man with eyes to drink in scenery and nature, and a soul to be stirred, fail to become one with the countryside?

Ornithology became a passion. My technique regarding Bird life was to make notes on scraps of paper of the colours and marks of the birds I spotted. Then I would look them up in a public library until, gradually, I became an expert on birds, holding many an enthralling conversation with ornithologists I met in the country. On occasions I was able to give them the locations of species and, once, I was mentioned in an article in a Bird-Watchers' magazine and referred to as 'Joe, a professional tramp with an amazing knowledge of bird life in the Lake District'. Not possessing a pair of binoculars, I often sat for hours on end on the Fells, watching buzzards soaring above me, rising and dipping seemingly oblivious to my presence, calling their sad song 'pee-oo pee-oo'. The buzzard's eyes are always searching the ground and this constant scrutiny was proved to me one evening when I had snared a rabbit for the pot. I placed it down on the grass whilst I raked up the flames of the fire and, turning, a buzzard was taking to the air with the rabbit in its beak. The raven, too, preys on small animals and its lusty wing-beating in flight is a joy to behold, but there is something eerie about the bird as well. But the peregrine falcon possesses a presence of majesty, a true king of the crags and a sovereign of the air, killing most of its meat on the wing. I studied kestrels and merlins, too, for the Fells are the haunt of the larger birds and although the smaller species are present they are scarce. I saw Nature in its cruelest moods on the Fells so for a softer side of the feathered world I would visit the streams and lakes along my route to watch the water birds – Great-Crested Grebes on Esthwaite Water, Little Grebes on Ullswater, Mute Swans, Tufted Ducks and Teal, Moorhens, Coots, Mallards and Cormorants, their sightings varying from lake to lake; the fast-moving streams provided the flashing colour of the Dipper with its white and chestnut chest dipping busily into the water for insect larvae; graceful Grey Wagtails, Yellow Wagtails delighted in their natural habitat whilst fraternising with visitors from the woodlands and dales, such as the Willow Warblers, Cock Redstarts, Chaffinches and Tits and many other birds, common and rare, who visited the banks of streams and the reedy areas of the tarns. I recorded my sightings and made notes of bird behaviour until I accumulated a pile of papers, which I tied together with string. I had a wild notion that one day I would write a Thesis on bird behaviour, but that was shattered, however, when I was caught in a cloudburst which almost succeeded in killing me by temporarily blinding me whilst on a hillside pitted by gullies and reduced my notes to pulp.

But my knowledge of Nature wasn't entirely gleaned from a desire to learn. Essentially, it was born out of necessity — the need to fill my belly. For weeks on end I would be away from towns. Your average tramp ate as much meat as he could beg, steal or 'borrow', but I learned to use the natural foods of the lanes and fields to supplement my diet. It was amazing the number of men who walked past acres of blackberries without picking the fruit. These and wild raspberries, rose-hips, nettles, hawthorn berries, elderberries, water-cress, comfrey, dandelions, horse-raddish — all these and many other plants and herbs I ate raw or made into stews and drinks and, by doing this during the warmer months, I believe that I built up a resistance to infection, a safeguard for the long winters spent in towns. Many times I cooked my favourite meal in a pot by the roadside and played host to passing travellers who would often be astounded when told they had eaten rabbit and nettle stew! Rabbits abounded then. Young nettle leaves taken from the top of the plant in May-time are delicious when boiled. I wasted very little, for rabbit skins would fetch a few coppers in the towns and, for a change of diet, there were always chicken runs handy for stealing 'one for the pot'. In the same way, I cooked all types of edible herbs, drinking the juice or using them for flavouring dishes such as partridge, pheasant and grouse when in season. So, if you add these game birds to the salmon and trout, eaten occasionally, you will see that the seasoned country tramp often lived well, paid nothing, and was partaking of more nourishing rich food than the cottagers and smallholders on whom he called.

Rum was only a few pence for a glass in those days and very popular with poachers and I caught many a grouse with it. The idea was to soak a few oats in the spirit and then spread them along the 'run' in a wood. Very few people except poachers have seen a drunken grouse, the rum acted like an anaesthetic and made the birds easy to deal with. Whilst the men with the shotguns were patiently waiting for the 12th August, many a poacher had had a surfeit of the meat.

But as any Lakeland dweller knows this area attracts a lot of rain. These wet spells could make life very tough indeed. Some days, even in the very middle of summer, rain poured down and I would be hard put to make a decision between starvation or pneumonia. To seek sanctuary at a farm often meant doing without food. But the years toughen a man and I suffered very little in the way of ill-health.

To be foot-loose and free amidst such wonderful country and not to sleep out under the stars was an affront to a beneficient Nature whose nocturnal sounds were music to the ears and eminently more acceptable to the snoring, grunting and coughing of the average doss-house. Being blessed with a sparsity of large towns, the area, consequently, had few vagrant dwellings but there was an abundance of farm buildings and barns, mainly for the asking, when I required a roof over my head. Up to 1935 the complicated Vagrancy Laws of England stated that any person found wandering abroad without visible means of support could be arrested, and this applied to all vagrants found kipping in barns, hen houses and such like dwellings. Afterwards, the Law was amended so that these vagrants were no longer classed 'rogues and vagabonds', provided they agreed to go to a lodging-house or some other accommodation selected by the police. This, in effect, meant very little and as tramps were a law unto themselves, the fact that they were now being given a choice before arrest did nothing to better their lot. When one considers that such trivial amendments were the only changes made to Acts passed in Medieval times it is plain that the treatment of vagrants was still primitive. The country 'bobby' used his own judgment over roadsters. He knew his men who were 'regulars' for the most part and, as long as they didn't cause trouble on his beat, then he left them alone when, in effect, he should have been arresting them for vagrancy if found with less than two shillings on their person.

There is still a deep-rooted belief in folk-lore amongst the older people, but in my day I was constantly hearing and experiencing the superstitions of the country folk. When the cock crowed this was a sign that strangers were on the way and often I would be told that I was expected when I arrived at a farmhouse. An old spinster who lived in a cottage close to Kirkstone Pass was a great believer in omens. One morning I happened to remark that I had seen magpies in the fields.

"How many didst see in my field?" she asked sharply.

"I'm not sure."

"Think!" she urged.

"At least ten," I said.

"Thar's going to cop it, then," she said seriously. "That's bad luck that is," and she repeated a rhyme I had heard many times:

One is for Sorrow
Two for Mirth
Three for a Wedding
Four for a Death
Five for Heaven, Six for Hell
But Seven's the devil's own sel . . .

"So, if you saw ten, Mester . . . !" She shook her head sadly.

I thought of how her cock always knew when I was about and wondered if she would be just as accurate. Fortunately good luck prevailed despite the omen!

I met folk who would never let the fire die, this was possible with turf and was a sure preventative against disease. Later, I learned from an old Lakeland character that the belief stemmed from an ancient belief that fire and smoke kept infection away.

When the milk wouldn't churn soil was brought from the nearest churchyard and placed in the byre and, despite protestations from clergymen, many old farming folk still persisted in this custom. I met wart charmers by the score and actually witnessed a 'before-and-after' cure. A young farm child had a painful wart on her foot so her grandmother buried a piece of steak as large as a saucer under a sod, then stuck a pin into the wart — ignoring the screams of the poor child — and then another pin was stuck into a tree close to the buried meat. The child was then commanded to address the tree thus:

Ash tree, Ash tree
Buy this wart from me.

I spent the night in the bracken-loft of the farm and the next morning the child came in to bring me a mug of tea and some toast. She had no fear of tramps, who had been a common sight to her since she was a baby. She cried —
"Look! Look! It's gone. The wart's gone!"
And, sure enough, it had gone. How it worked I don't know, but I believe fear had a large part to play in it and as many complaints are of a psychological origin, fear instilled into a sufferer by many of the old 'cures' would often bring about a seemingly miraculous recovery. Horse urine was once offered to me by a lowland drover when I complained of pain in my legs.
"You don't drink it, mate, you rub it in," he explained, but I still declined.
Hot cow-pats for inflammation was another 'certain' remedy though some believers swore by them applied cold. Bee stings for rheumatic pain and raw onions for keeping colds at bay, the logic being that no bug known to man could survive in an onion. One superstition looked on with great favour by me was that it meant a year's bad luck to refuse a cup of tea to a tramp!
I heard the passing bell tolled, a custom which has now ceased. After the death the church bell was rang, the number of tolls indicating the sex of the deceased. The pattern altered depending on the area, but the most usual was six bells for a man, four for a woman and three for a child.
Sometimes I would take wild remote tracks across the

Fells in order to shorten my journeys to certain villages to put in an hour's house-calling before it was time to bed down for the night. In bygone days these tracks were known as corpse roads, the gruesome name coming from their use as roads for the transportation of the dead by pack-horses. Once I walked from Wasdale Head to Eskdale over Burn Moor. It was not a happy walk; despite my fondness for the area depression hung over me as I trudged. Simply, the eeriness of remote places of course, but I was left in no doubt by a whiskery old chap I met in Eskdale that it was due to tramping across haunted territory for the moor is said to be haunted by a galloping horse carrying a coffin. Legend has it that a young man died, was placed in his coffin and transported by horse across the moor on the corpse road. A heavy mist descended. The horse bolted, being lost to sight, and there was nothing that could be done but return home and hope that when the mist cleared the horse and coffin would be found. The dead lad's mother was so overcome with grief that she died from the shock. So she, in turn, was placed in a coffin and once more they set out for the churchyard, the horse bearing the boy's coffin still lost. By this time it was snowing and the second horse bolted. The local folk say it fell down a crag and was buried under the snow. Then the first horse was found and the boy buried in a churchyard, but his mother's body was never recovered and, according to legend, the horse still roams the moor carrying her coffin.

I laughed at the tale, much to the annoyance of the teller. "You'd best be gettin' thee tea from t'missis, mester, then off with thee before it's dark. A young hiker in a public house scoffed at the tale only last year – day after he were found dead at foot of a crag. It don't do to laugh at legends, mester."

'The glad day breaking on the road you're taking and the world's a land of song. That's the hour you cherish for your cares all perish as you gaily march along' – so sang the baritone of the 'Gay Highway' – the Road. But not always was it the romantic highway so popular with lyricists, for the road is a hard task-master and a man has to learn its lessons. Retrospect is a great softening force to the hard reality of memory, but in all truth I can say that the Lakes represented to me the gay highway. As a professional traveller, never did I enjoy any journeys as much as those made in the Lakes. I found the people friendly and the roads held an abundance of colour, especially the stretch from Windermere to Ambleside, the northerly curve of the boomerang-shaped Lake Windermere. That road was an arena for the eccentricities of the motley crew who trod it; there was Aberdeen Glen and his partner Glasgow Baldy, two Scottish tramps — one of them walking backwards and intermittently playing the bagpipes — both dressed in full Highland regalia; the only kilted tramps I ever saw. Another old chap, wearing a top hat, wheeled a gramophone around with him in a pram. It was one of the large horn varieties, so valuable today as collectors' items, and when played its strident tones were guaranteed to bring the cottagers to their gates, the basin of the pram making an excellent collection plate for thrown coins. He only had two records as long as I knew him, one the Grand March from Aida and the other, played only on Sundays, was Abide with Me. Needless to say, Sunday was by far his best day for business.

Then there was 'Sir Henry Barratt' who lived in henhouses and went around repairing mats and basket-chairs. He regularly sat on a wall with his repair kit alongside him singing at the top of his voice. He was an apple-cheeked leprechaun-like little chap with ever the backside out of his trousers in perfect mockery of the world of sartorial fashion; and not only did his posterior protrude but so did two most grotesque bunions. 'Henry' suffered agonies with his feet. Good feet were essential to the tramp and he must have endured untold punishment, so cutting the toes out of his shoes was the only way he could walk, if his floundering gait could be described as walking. Known disrespectfully amongst the brotherhood as the 'Pregnant Duck', he was also known to all and sundry as Sir Henry Barratt the man who appeared in the famous shoe advertisements.

Feet! God knows how the tramp needed a good pair. An old roadster gave me a tip early on in my career and I never neglected his advice. Every day I bathed them in running brook water, dried them well, then gave them a vigorous rubbing with Docken leaves until the skin was green. Whenever I could buy it or barter it, I would rub whisky into the soles. Methylated spirits (a much more common commodity on the road than whisky) worked the same way. My feet became hard and ever afterwards I never suffered a corn or a blister. Sometimes I would rub a raw onion into the skin until the juice was absorbed. Fortunately, I am 'stock-size', to quote the jargon of the shoe trade, so when it came to a gift of a pair of shoes I was often fortunate and able to vary my footwear. Not like poor Tapper Regan, a noted Westmorland beggar, who took size 12 and usually had to settle for the agony of a pair of size 9s or 10s, consequently giving a look of genuine pain which actually furthered his cause.

The Ambleside lodging-house was noted for its exorbitant charge — a shilling a night when I knew it. However, there was a brace of ladies who were filled with the milk of human kindness and supplied the doss-money when a man hadn't got it. The system worked this way and was typical of the way many charitable organisations acted. The women had a financial arrangement with the police whereby roadsters, after giving an account of themselves and satisfying the sergeant that they were, indeed, penniless, could collect a chit which was then presented to the lodging-house keeper and subsequently redeemed by the beneficent ladies. I hope by now that the reader will have sufficient knowledge of the tramp's character to understand that the tale told to the police was usually a false one, for often he would hide his money under a stone or in a field then retrieve it once he had got the chit.

The tramp-house was in Bridge Street and known, except to residents of the street, as 'Rattleghyll'. As Ghyll is a Lakeland word for a fast-moving stream the nickname must have arisen from the noise made by the stream. However, having stayed on several occasions in 'Rattleghyll' doss-house, I can confirm that the 'rattle' part of the name perfectly fitted the consumptive coughing of the occupants. I heard the death-rattle so often it became a commonplace sound.

It was during a wild, wet night in Ambleside that I had a frightening experience. It is often said that following the seemingly endless road can drive a man insane; indeed, there were mad men who wandered the land unchecked – dangerous men, escapees from lunatic asylums. Every time a man entered a doss-house or 'spike' he was taking a risk even though he may have visited thousands and not been in danger but, like me, he could be unfortunate only once, which was quite sufficient. Luckily, I survived to tell the tale. It was time for bed. The bell clanged for the third time which was the final warning that the kitchen had to be emptied of its human furniture or else it meant the street. Only one man remained as I left the kitchen. He was mumbling to himself. I had been lying on the flock mattress which served as a bed for a few minutes when I suddenly decided that I could do with a drink of water. As there was a convenient wash-room I took my drum and went in search of it along the dark corridor. The gas mantles had been extinguished yet I saw two lights – suspended lights – not the lights of gas jets or torches. If they had been just above ground-level I would have taken them for cat's eyes. I suddenly felt afraid, not certain, in that split second of panic, whether to rush to the wash-room or to the sleeping quarters. Then hot breath was on my lips. A fetid smell in my nostrils. My rib cage was being crushed and my senses were deserting me, the great pressure made struggle impossible and I was slipping away over a yawning ravine – then I heard drumming, pounding feet, muffled curses. I tasted spirit on my lips – brandy. Brandy in a doss-house! The deputy's flask was a comfort. "Another few seconds and that mad devil would have killed you. He'll not get in here again, that's for sure. He's a bloody loony I tell you." Ever afterwards I searched the faces in every doss-house I visited for that ginger head and the mad flaming eyes. I never forgot.

Above Ambleside, up and over the tortuous Kirkstone Pass and beyond the craggy terrain skirting it, one arrives, weary and thirsty, at Brotherswater. Here I would bathe after the grind of that cruel Pass, a road I had no option but to take if I wanted to reach profitable trading areas northwards. One August night the heat was stifling and I was worn out after the slog over the Pass. I ate a delicious rabbit stew which I had cooked over a wood fire by the lake side. A beautiful summer's evening when a man feels contentment of mind, a full stomach, and the body longing to succumb to a sleep invited by the heady wood smoke — the holiday-maker would have succumbed, but I knew the danger of such folly, waking cold and shivering, covered in dew, for the nights can suddenly turn very cold in Lakeland. So, I wandered off with my belongings to a deserted barn over Hartsop way. There was bracken on the floor for it was a regular abode of road men. I gladly flung myself down and was soon asleep. Early sunshine through the slits in the roof had me awake and by my side was another body. I wasn't alarmed for it was obviously a colleague of the road, but I was far too tired to investigate further so I simply turned over and went back to sleep. When next I awoke the sun was strong; Kirkstone Pass had made me sore and my leg muscles throbbed. I yawned and saw the other tramp lying next to me. He was still, too still it seemed to me. I turned him over and his face was deathly white, his hands like ice to my fingers. I had slept cheek by jowl with a corpse the whole night long. Old tramps had to die somewhere and their discovery in such a place was not a rarity so I gathered my belongings together and hit the Pass road northwards for the village of Patterdale. I saw no point in getting involved in something which I knew nothing about. Some shepherd or sheltering walker would find him. From this village beneath the crags and fells one follows the crooked-arm shape of majestic Ullswater northwards and I never failed to pass a night in the disused Greenside Mine beneath Sheffield Pike. It was warm and dry with little chance of disturbance but, first, I always took the precaution of lighting a rush torch to make sure I was alone, having the presence of mind, however, not to wander too far into gas-filled cavities with a naked flame. Baldy Crab, a decrepit old vagrant, lost all his hair by doing just that and news travelled fast on the grapevine so that the boys learned from the misfortunes of others.

The dread people felt for tramps was my protection, especially at night, so consequently I was left to my own devices. But not so one night when a young chap wheeling a bicycle approached me as I was settling down for the night on a grassy slope above a river. It was rarely that I slept out in the open, conditions had to be good and this site was ideal for it was protected from the wind by a row of trees. The young chap obviously had the same idea.

"Good evening," he greeted me. "I see you are going to camp here, so it must be a good spot for a man like you knows the best places." It was meant as a compliment. "Can I join you?" he added, politely.

"I've no objection," I told him. In fact, I was very pleased for he had a packet of sandwiches which he shared and I made a drum of tea and we had a very pleasant conversation about life in general.

"This is the life," said the young chap as he lay back with a sigh after the meal.

"All right for holidaymakers," I laughed. "But what do you think to making your living on the road? Different tale then." Inadvertently, I had given him the lead for which he had been angling, for he had asked me veiled questions about my life travelling in the Lakes.

"That's what I'd like to ask you. I'm a reporter on a Weekly Magazine and I'm on a cycling holiday, but I've got the idea of doing a story on tramps. How they live and travel, you know the sort of thing. I believe I'm what Shaw called a middle-class tramp fancier."

I was game, for I could see no reason for refusing an eager lad but, first of all, I took the particulars of his magazine and his name and address, whereupon he assured me that a postal order would be sent to Penrith Post Office. He fired questions and I answered, giving him full licence for the 'romantic' side of the life he was obviously seeking. His readers were a middle-class sophisticated set whose taste was for the more attractive side of life — even the tramp's; so, with unbridled hyperbole, I recited a highly varnished account of my day-to-day 'adventures', omitting the boring routine of what was to me a job like anyone else's, and made myself into a swashbuckling knight of the road. However, he was not taken in as much as I thought. We slept near one another on the grass and he was still fast asleep when I left the camp site at an early hour, but he was obviously no man's fool for his cycle was padlocked to his ankle! Nevertheless, he was as good as his word for on my next journey I called at Penrith G.P.O. and collected a £2 Postal Order.

In Pooley Bridge I made a shilling by selling recipes to tourists for a penny a sheet. In Ambleside Library I had written out a recipe for a blackberry dessert on sheets of paper I had collected from the wastepaper baskets. A farmer's wife had given me the recipe but little did she realise that I would be peddling it around for years, always a good line and I copied out and sold many a hundred. I headed the recipe 'BLACKBERRY SUPREME - A method for using up windfall apples or pears: In large pan boil windfall fruit in half-pint of water. Do not peel or core fruit. Add 1 pound blackberries. Boil until fruit has fallen. Strain contents through muslin into bowl. To the purée add sugar to taste and 3 tablespoons of gelatine. When set eat with cream.' I never tasted the dish myself, but that recipe brought me in pounds over the years. New ideas for money-making were constantly being considered in my mind, the majority either too risky or not worth the effort. Once I even made up poetry and sold it, but I wasn't much of a rhymer and soon ran out of ideas. But the Cabbage Trick was my *pièce de résistance* but, like most con tricks, one couldn't repeat it too often in the same place. Penrith was the farthest point of my ramblings and a good town for street selling and, like Kendal, being on the main trunk road between Scotland and England it attracted a large floating population. Happening to chance on a Market Gardener's tool shed for a night's kip, I was up before the gardeners arrived for work the next day and had time to inspect the plot. I found a box of young cabbage plants so, choosing a dozen of the choicest, I set off with them wrapped in a wet rag for the town centre. By midmorning I had sold the plants to a rather prim lady at sixpence for the dozen, which was very expensive, but seeing that I offered to plant them into the bargain she didn't quibble. I chose midday as the ideal time to go to the house – dinner time – and I made a great show of bedding the plants most diligently and watering them. The woman could hardly deny me a cup of tea and a plate of meat sandwiches after that, plus an extra threepence for my trouble. She thanked me profusely for my kindness and I went off about other business in the town. When darkness fell I was back at the woman's garden where I dug up the plants again and placed them in the wet rag ready for resale the next day. I worked the trick five times that week, once getting a huge meal of home-cured bacon and cabbage for my efforts. Fellow lotus-eaters loved to compare tricks of the trade and ever afterwards I was known among them as 'Cabbage', and my tale had many an airing. In Pooley Bridge I was caught red-handed on the return journey. Obviously my trickery had preceded me. A torch shone into my face as I dug up plants at midnight and I spent the rest of the night in the local police station cell. Expecting to be up at Penrith Petty Sessions the next morning, I was very surprised to be let off with a telling off from the police sergeant. He did his best to be severe with me but I'm sure that underneath the official look of authority there was a little gremlin trying its best to make him laugh. This was a means of making an illegal living he had not come across before!

10

SUMMER BUMMING

One moonlit night I bivouacked beneath a railway bridge close to Souter Fell. It was a one-track line and I knew that no trains ran at night. Moonlight can be eerie and although I was accustomed to night sounds, when the countryside comes alive with a symphony of hooting, droning, screeching and the rataplan of wings, on this particular night I almost began to believe the stories of hobgoblins and poltergeists, said to haunt the Fells and Valleys at night time. Put a man in the right circumstances and his preconceived convictions can melt like snow in a heat wave. The old tea drum I had used for years had eventually sprung a leak and I had replaced it with a large tin can, which would have to suffice until I could afford another tin mug. I was nodding off to sleep when I was startled by a clanging noise. Whatever had caused it was very close at hand. Assuming that some animal was on the prowl, I went back to sleep only to be awakened by another similar noise. A sharp metallic sound. I began to suspect that some local wag had discovered my whereabouts and was trying to scare me. I climbed up on to the road, but there was no one to be seen, the moonlight revealing only the fields and the nearby Fell side. Once more I fell asleep and yet again the same sound occurred. I was frightened. Yes, for the first time for many a long time I admit I was frightened. And then the moonlight penetrated the tunnel in a shaft of light, and all was revealed. With a threshing of wings, a large bird swooped below the bridge and bit the tin can with its beak. I recognised it as a Tawny Owl. The mystery solved, I reprimanded myself for being afraid and gladly fell back to sleep.

The incident fascinated me and the next morning I recounted it to an old chap who was leaning on a gate at the foot of Souter Fell.

"An owl it may bin, lad, but I tell thi as place is 'aunted. Phantoms and such lak." He had a pipe in his hand and dug me in the chest with the stem for emphasis. There was something so grave about the old man that I asked him if he had ever seen a ghost.

"Ghosts, lad? Have I ever sin a ghost? Nat just one, lad, I've sin thousands on 'em — oh, tha' can smile, lad. Phantom it wer. Hes ta ner heerd o' Phantom Army o' Souter Fell?"

I had to admit that I had not.

"Well, it wer in't Seventeen hundreds. Scooers o'fowk see it then. In't sky tha knows, legions o'marchin' men, columns of horses. Well, I see t'same thing twenty year sen. Same as it's written in't library books — just t'same. A gradely army gooin' t'war. Haafe an hour they wor passing."

"Where abouts was it?" I asked

He pointed across the Fell land to the very top. "On t' skyline."

"And did anyone else see it?" I queried.

"Aye, owd Billy Cronty, he's deead now. Ah reckon it's like a photograph teken bi t'sky, and then on certain days when conditions are reet it shows up. It mud 'appen bod once in a lifetime. But it dud 'appen, I see it mesel'. Mind you, ah ner med owt out on it. Bear in mind another owd mon see it afooer me, but they bod laughed at him — — legions o'men there wor an' wi' weapons an' armour. Shiny, like silver, it wor an' gret plumes on th' horses heyds."

"Why didn't you tell the papers? You might have got paid for the story."

"What, an' be t'laughing stock o't place? Nay. If it hed bin sin bi a crowd o'fowk, like it wor afooer, it wod a bin aw reet. But ween it's bod a couple o'chaps as hev sin it, then that meks a difference. They mud think Ah wer a crank or a liar and Ah want no reporters coming here axing questions. Me an' Owd Cronty see it an' Ah'm sticking to it."

I left the old chap mumbling to himself. Later, I checked in reference books about the sighting in the Eighteenth Century and, sure enough, many people are reputed to have been eye-witnesses to the same scene described so vividly by the old chap. There were no accounts of more recent sightings and I have often wondered if the old chap actually did see the Phantom Army, or was he an even better exponent of the lying tale than I was?

On all my Lakeland treks the westerly course of my eventual journey southwards would be from Penrith through Greystone Pillar, New Biggin, wending my way by short cuts across moorland and scrub to Penruddick, where I was sure of a warm welcome from a farmer who would give me a couple of days' work for a fair wage. From here I would take the main road, good both for the comfort of the feet and profitable scrounging. And so to Keswick, picturesque on the northern shore of Derwentwater along whose easterly shore I followed a road which offered the finest views of lake and fell land. To hurry on such a walk was a sin, the hand of the Master painter had laid such colours of wilderness and water-mood on His canvas that even the rattle of the coins at the day's end took second place to the feeling of privilege this enchanted place left upon one. One passes such delightfully named places as Hogs Earth and Shepherd Crag and, gazing back, mighty Skiddaw looks down in bald majesty upon Keswick, a noble backcloth of dignified mountain, the fourth highest in Britain, a mountain apart from its Lakeland brothers with their peerless crags and fearsome gorges. To me it is the friendly mountain, the softer side of a fierce, but beautiful, part of England. I heard it described as the grandmother of mountains, a remark not meant to reflect credit on it as a man's mountain, for it is notably easy to climb. It is a tiger with its teeth drawn, but let brave men strive to conquer the rockiest, precipitous heights of their own choice, and I will be content to watch the sunshine playing a game of light and shade on this, the good-humoured mountain. Crossing beneath the Lake Road from Keswick, above Rosthwaite, is Stonethwaite beck which joins the River Derwent to drain into Derwentwater at the highest shoulder of Great Bay.

September was well advanced as I approached the outskirts of Borrowdale. I was sore and hungry, desperately in need of dry clothes, for the summer had been an extremely wet one. Painfully plodding it, I hoped for luck in Borrowdale. The sound of surging water had battered my eardrums for hours on end, fields were flooded and, often, I had to wade through swirling waters. But above the sound of the Beck at Rosthwaite I heard a distinctive sound, one of dire distress. The frightened bleating of a sheep. Mounting a wall, I saw a sheep standing on a rock in the middle of the swollen stream. With the rain pouring down the stream was rapidly rising with the volume of water tumbling from the crags above and there seemed no chance for the animal. I decided on a rescue operation. I was soaked to the skin anyway and that sheep could be my way to a good hot dinner and a change of clothes. So ran the train of my thoughts. Plunging through the sodden land and dripping bracken, I headed into the water and soon I was knee deep. Inch by inch I progressed towards the sheep. The stupid creature panicked when it saw me, slithering and sliding on the shiny rock. At last, thigh deep, I leaned out to grasp it. Those few yards back were like miles as the animal kicked and struggled in my grip but, holding on for dear life, I got it to safety. Standing in the shallow water in a pair of wellingtons was a young boy.

"That was brave, mester," he said. "Reet brave, mester."

"Is it your sheep?" I asked, hoping it belonged to his family.

"No, but it's belonging Owd Ned yonder what farms on't crags. It's his ewe. By, but that were reet brave, mester. Come on, I'll tek thee to Ned — 'appen he'll gie thi some food."

Full of my amazing rescue, the young boy gabbled away as he led me up the fell towards a craggy-looking farmhouse which stood stark on the skyline. There was something cold and unfriendly about the place. At last we reached it and Ged, as the lad was called, knocked on the door, which was opened by the farmer himself. My heart sank at the sight of him.

"What does want, lad?" was the rough greeting.

Ged told the man what I had done, emphasising how I had waded up to my thighs in the deeper water. Genuinely the lad wanted to help me and his pleas would have drawn blood from a stone, but not hospitality from Ned.

"Weer's sheep, then?" was the curt enquiry.

"It's safe on good grassland," said Ged. "I see him with me own eyes. He saved your ewe, mester. Let him in and give him some food. Tha's got some owd clothes 'appen?"

"He's a tramp. I know't breed on 'em. He's fooled thi, lad." Old Ned made to push the door shut, but persistent little Ged put his foot in the door and shouted, "He saved thi ewe, skinflinting owd sod! He saved thi ewe, I tell thi! I hope thi drown in thi own spit!"

There were tears in the little kid's eyes and as we walked back down the fell he told me he lived with an Aunt who detested tramps. But he'd find a way and when I told him I would be trudging on towards Borrowdale he ran off home. I was almost in the village when I heard a familiar voice. It was Ged, furiously pedalling a very tall cycle, his short legs barely reaching the pedals.

"I've brought thi some grub, mester." He tossed me a bag which contained two meat sandwiches and a large lump of mouldy cheese. I sat in a bus shelter to eat it and that mouldy cheese was as good as a beef steak. I had always found farmers tight when it came to money, particularly Fell men. They earned it the hard way and parting with it was a personal bereavement. But Old Ned was the true scrooge of Dickensian stature and somehow kindly little Ged ever afterwards reminded me of Tiny Tim. I hope he wasn't found out by his Aunt. But in the main farmers and smallholders were kindly when it came to giving shelter and food and Old Ned was an exception.

When I first had the notion of putting my tramping experiences to paper I asked myself which was the most outstanding memory of all. Standing out above the rest was one which I realised would not sound true in an autobiography. It smacked of fabled romance, yet it happened and I can only repeat the age-old saying that truth is sometimes stranger than fiction and leave it at that.

It happened outside Borrowdale also. A middle-aged man lived in a large stone-faced house, obviously the residence of a man of some means and, naturally, it became a calling place for the roadsters. I once heard he was a retired banker, but never knew for sure although philanthropist he certainly was. This particular summer, 'thirty-three' if my memory serves me correctly, was a good one and I was in a vastly better state than when I had saved the ewe a year or so previously. I was passing the gate of the house when the owner, in plus-fours, came out in rather an agitated state.

"Are you in a hurry?" he asked me.

"Not particularly, sir," I answered politely.

"Good. Then will you be kind enough to join me and some more of your comrades of the road in some lunch?" he made it sound as if I would be doing him a favour if I accepted. I didn't disappoint him. "I think this calls for a little explanation . . . what's your name, by the way?"

"Joe."

"Joe, yes, I must explain before we go in. My housekeeper is just making the tea so you timed your arrival well. I was expecting company, you see, a few chaps from town up for the grouse, with their wives. Well, I wrote to invite them to join me for lunch. My housekeeper went to great trouble to prepare a cold buffet lunch — smoked salmon and all the trimmings. They turned up an hour ago and refused the lunch, saying they had dined at Ambleside. Must say I was jolly cross, showed it, too, I'm sure, and Mrs Jordan was in tears. She loves to put on a real spread, you know. Well, I sent 'em all off with a flea in their ears and when I looked on all that lovely food I said to myself, 'I'll do what the chap in the Bible did. I'll go into the highways and byeways and fetch 'em in'. Toffee-nosed lot of devils they are anyhow. My table's not good enough for 'em, hey? Well, I'll show 'em, so I went out and found a couple of wandering chaps in the village. You'll join us now. Come on, my son, this is your lucky day!"

A pram, covered by a dirty sack, was parked by the door. "Belongs to one of the lads," I was told.

Imagine the scene — first, a large ornate room, delightfully furnished with a huge Welsh dresser dominating one wall, exquisitely carved tables and chairs, richly upholstered arm-chairs and deep-piled Persian carpet. To my eyes something out of the Arabian Nights — but in bizzare, almost alarming, contrast, seated on the plush chairs, were two of the scruffiest men I had ever seen, and I had met plenty. I recognised Blinker Davies, a notorious poultry thief, so named because of a defect in his eyesight which made him blink when he talked. He had a brown shoe on one foot and a black one on the other, and was clad in an ancient red dressing-gown he had salvaged from some dustbin, judging by its decrepit state. Lounging back in style, he was puffing on a **king-size Havana and intermittently sipping an apéritif**, his long ginger hair draping over the antimacassar on the couch. Opposite to him was Redstone Bill, a humped-backed character who hawked red stone he picked on the seashore and wheeled it around in an ancient pram. He simply wore a tattered shirt and a pair of multi-coloured corduroy breeches and odd boots which gave no lie to the mileage he claimed to cover in a year. He was perched on the edge of a chair, eagerly anticipating the arrival of the food and meanwhile drinking beer out of a bottle. And what a spread the grouse-shooters had missed — three trolleys laden with eatables were wheeled to the centre of the floor by the housekeeper who handed us a plate apiece. Our host was delighted at the way we wolfed down his lunch. It was obvious I had run across an eccentric with a weird sense of humour who was perfectly at ease amongst us and accepted our rough manners, treating us as equals. After we had stuffed ourselves we discussed everything under the sun, including politics, over a bottle of port.

I knew Blinker was an out-and-out blackguard, but a plausible rogue for all that and popular with the farmers who never realised it was often him, and not the foxes, who stole their poultry during the night. Now he was going red in the face with the unaccustomed port and airing his views in a manner which made me want to crawl away and hide under the table. Here we were being entertained in a style only the strata of High Society knew in those days, yet Blinker seemed oblivious of this as he set about a blistering attack on the class our host represented, calling them parasites on the working classes and bloated money grabbers, blaming them for the General Strike and saying that Oswald Moseley would give them their just deserts when he got into power. England would be run on the way of things in Russia and the working class would rule and it was God help the money-bags — and so on. How our host sat there calmly I don't know; I would have grabbed him by the scruff of the neck and thrown him out of the house. Job was certainly this man's patron. Gradually, after what seemed like an age of insults, I turned the subject round to Nature and found that Mr Shuttleworth (I call him that for convenience's sake) was a keen butterfly collector. He showed me his collection and whilst we were in his library I tried to apologise for Blinker's behaviour. He would hear none of it and said he didn't blame him and I often think of his words which, when considered in the relevance of the times — 1934, were meaningful. "I don't blame him. If I was in his shoes I'd think the same. We have long prided ourselves on being captains of industry, trouble is there are far too many captains and not enough ordinary working men."

After discussing his collection, we went back to the dining-room to find Blinker and Redstone Bill snoring their heads off. I was surprised to find Blinker still there because, only for the port, he would have been on his way with some of the silverware I didn't doubt. Several times afterwards I called at the house where I always got tea and some food, but never again did I ever experience anything like the amazing luncheon party when Mr Shuttleworth went into the highways and byeways to find his guests.

Borrowdale holds many memories, one of which again concerns Blinker Davies. Blinker was a true Lakes tramp, not for him the wandering role like most of us. He was born and bred in Lakeland, Broughton-in-Furness to be exact. In trouble with the police for most of his youth, he was kicked out of the house by his family who were downright ashamed of him with his criminal record and his terms in several prisons. But Blinker didn't move far away, simply cadging for a living without moving out of Cumberland. Like all nomads, he was cute and knew the best 'marks'. Only a mile or two from Borrowdale an old sheepman lived in a little tin-roofed shack. Once, before his wife died, it was kept clean and provided a decent home for the couple, but when she died the old man let the place go to rack and ruin. He simply lived in the kitchen and never went into the other rooms. Rumour had it that he had plenty of money, but local folks looked on him as a 'crackpot' and the kids as a figure of fun. One night, down in the pub, he took pity on a hiker who was looking for accommodation and invited him to spend the night at his house. Not really having much choice on a filthy night, the hiker went home with the old man, despite the comments of the customers about the state of the house. The hiker, despite his 'Oxford' accent, only grinned and said it would be an experience. What happened after that became a great tale in the pubs for miles around. The young gentleman was rather staggered to find that the locals hadn't exaggerated the filthy state of the house, but nevertheless he accepted the offer of the use of the bedroom. He groped his way in the dark leaving the old chap sitting in a chair by the fire. Managing to find the bed, he crawled inside some coverings and lay there trying to console himself that anything was better than being out in the pouring rain. But hardly had he stretched himself out when there was a great shout and he felt someone kicking him. He was out of bed in a flash, followed by his bed mate who was recognisable to the old man as none other than Blinker Davies. The hiker obviously took him for less than mortal and sped off into the wet night, never to return. Blinker was evicted with the aid of a poker. Afterwards, Blinker revealed that he had used the old shack for three months without being detected by the old chap who had never been into the bedroom since his wife died. Blinker had gone there in search of money, found none, but discovered an ideal place to sleep at night instead.

    From Borrowdale I would desert the mundane pursuits of daily life and head away from trodden routes of everyday traffic, away for the Borrowdale Fells, over Bessyfoot, White Crag, following Longstrath Beck and its offshoots towards Langdale Fell and Pike of Stickle, with its hidden loot, stumbling past sheep and hare, skirting the site of the Ancient Axe Factory, so well excavated and searched for relics of pre-historic axes; this was my holiday region – this tramps' terrain for relaxing on these wild Fells, by becks and tarns, I studied Nature, collected wild flowers, and existed in hermit fashion on provisions I had saved, out in the open or, in extremely bad weather, I copied the hermits of legend and slept in a cave. But a man had to make a living and back I would go to the profitable roads and the grimmer side of my character. I feel I can claim to have been a competent tramp but I would never have made a hermit for I was too fond of my stomach.

I have quite a remarkable memory of the Ancient Langdale Axe Factory. One day whilst idly burrowing amongst the rubble and scree for rock plants, I came across a stone object resembling an axe head. Not having the slightest notion of what the site had once been, I put it in my tattered sack and forgot all about it. All tramps were collectors of nondescript items and it was quite amazing how often these odd things would come in useful. But in the case of the axe, it remained in the bottom of the sack for at least a year until one wild winter's day, when I was on a road somewhere between Knaresbrough and York; extreme hunger and cold had been my companion for many hours, trudging through the night in the teeth of a gale. I saw men queueing outside a small village shop and I recognised them as Casual Ward tramps. Questioning one I found that they were claiming food against tickets given to them at York Workhouse. This was the method used by some spikes. "You ain't got no tally, mate, so you'll get no victuals," I was told but, being so hungry, I determined to try my luck. For a change, I told the truth to the shop-keeper who seemed a decent sort of chap. He listened patiently to my tale.

"Well, you're honest anyway," was his reaction to my appeal for food. "Tell you what, leave me something useful out of your sack and I'll give you the same as the Workhouse lads — eight ounces of bread and two ounces of cheese."

Manna from Heaven just then. I knew he was testing me, so I emptied the contents of the sack on the floor — sodden items of clothing and the stone axe head.

Almost a year to the day I was in the village again, my circumstances somewhat better, and I wanted to thank him for his kindness. His face beamed a welcome.

"Well, I'm delighted to see you. Never dreamed you'd show up, not being one of the regulars." This greeting surprised me and what he said next flabbergasted me. "Remember the axe head you left me for the food? Well one of the lads from the spike saw it one day and reckoned it was valuable. Said he was a student of ancient implements. Now, I didn't trust the chap, I'll be honest with you, but it shows how wrong you can be sometimes. I gave it to him to find out the value and do you know he turned up a month later with fifteen quid and a letter to prove he'd sold it to a dealer for that much. I took a fiver, gave him one and here's yours. If you hadn't turned up I was going to split it with him."

I spent ten shillings on food and left the shop feeling like a millionaire, hardly able to believe such amazing luck.

For though I confess to being an incurable romantic, mention of the Pike of Stickle and its Axe Factory always brings memories flooding back of the beast I made of myself on that fiver which somewhat overcomes its geological interest!

The Fells are grand in their own way, but the softer regions, the valleys and the pasture lands, represent the warmer side of nature. There is no more tranquil sight than the Village Green; they come in all shapes and sizes, unique to their own particular setting, and I took my leisure on hundreds of them, but none took my fancy more than the tiny green at Elterwater where visitors washed down their sandwiches with beer brought at the pub alongside. Here you got beer served from a bucket. It is said that a tramp christened this delightful Lake hamlet centuries ago when he called at a house to beg a drink, but he was refused with a rebuff, "There's plenty o'watter in't lake!" said the woman gruffly.

"Hell to water!" said the tramp in disgust and, so the locals claim, ever afterwards the place had been known as Elterwater. There is a vast fund of these stories to be found in the Lake District, still told to this day by the locals with a relish that their original author could not have bettered. They are proud of their heritage.

From here I followed the roads heading south through the wooded valley which lies between the Fells of Skelwith to the south-west and Longrigg to the north-east, a soft country of trees, warm colours and dancing becks where the sheep lent a pastoral shade to contrast higher reaches of rugged terrain for the wanderer and a happy hunting ground amongst the warm-hearted sheep farmers; then onwards to Hawkshead of ancient history, cobwebbed by time to hold in its environs a magical aura of the England of our forefathers. Such a place is steeped in legend and my favourite is the tale of the 'Drunken Duck' pub.

The wife of the landlord of this ancient inn found what appeared to be a dead duck in the inn yard. She plucked it in readiness for the oven then laid it on a slab. Upon returning a few hours later she was astonished to see the bald duck squawking and flapping its wings in the yard. The mystery was solved when it was discovered that a barrel of ale had sprung a leak and the duck had partaken of several pints. The woman was so upset that she knitted a jersey of Hawkshead wool for the duck, which it wore until its feathers grew again.

It was at Hawkshead that I met Prince Barkendyne 'the king of the buskers' as his placard, which he wore on his back, proclaimed. When I met him he was past his prime of musicianship, but he still sang well and squeezed a melodious tune out of a battered old squeeze-box. My singing in a pub must have attracted him for he came into the bar and gave us a tune then accompanied me whilst I sang. We got a good night's beer out of it and later that night, as we kipped in a barn, I agreed to break my usual routine of repeating the Lakes journey and the next day we set out for Morecambe. Old Sol did us proud, the sands were packed with trippers and holiday-makers and two tramps made money while he shone. The Prince, who told fortunes as a sideline, was attired in a wide white straw hat from which hung tiny bells; a red shirt and a green cravat gave him a bohemian gypsy look which suited his act of singing to the accordian. The 'thirties decade produced scores of characters like the 'Prince' — in my lifetime, certainly, it was the most colourful period — they were larger than life, outrageous characters who added a little glamour at a time when this commodity was scarce, all the more attractive because they contrasted with the drabness of the times. His patter always began with a recital of his own history in which he claimed to be descended from royal stock, the rightful claimant to the title 'Prince'. Some rogue somewhere along the line had cheated his branch of the Barkendyne family and, instead of living in opulence, he was forced to sing and tell fortunes for his living. But he would get even, justice would be done — the Barkendynes would be a force again; he knew, he saw it in the palms of his hands — "Now if any lady or gentleman would care to know *their* fortune, just place a silver coin in the hand of Prince Barkendyne, and I'll tell you what life holds for you —" A street entertainer had to be versatile, for people got to know them well over the years and so if a man could vary his performance he made a better collection. The Prince was dressed for the part he played therefore my more trampish image, coupled with an above-average baritone voice, gave him the idea of using me as a 'sob mooch', a tramp word having several meanings but in this case a man who sang songs to appeal to the masses, to play on the emotions. For the 'thirties was an era of sad songs given birth by the grim times. He had a song which not only spoke of hardship but of man's determination to overcome it and we rehearsed it until he considered I was singing it with the required amount of pathos and feeling sufficient to melt the hearts of John Public into digging deep into his pockets for a couple of 'genuine lads' out to beat all that life could throw at them in the way of hardship. It was called 'The Dusty Road' and I sang it so often I have never forgotten the words:

> *Got no money, got no cheque,*
> *All this worry is bendin' my back.*
> *But I got to keep going, can't turn back.*
> *Got to keep totin' this load.*
>
> *I'm just fumbling through the dark,*
> *Grumblin', mumblin' as I walk.*
> *Heaven help me, you're my prayer.*
> *Show me the end of this road.*
>
> *Nobody knows what a load I'm bearin',*
> *Nobody cares if it's rags I'm wearin',*
> *Nobody says — 'Brother let me share your troubles'*
> *Travelling on a dusty road!*

Footin' it along, though I sweat and swelter,
Singing a song 'til I reach the Delta,
Out in a storm, not a friend to seek for shelter
On a dusty road.

Swamps to the right of me!
Swamps to the left of me!
Blue skies I never see.
Though the road looks black
I'll never turn back.
Pray to Heaven for my Destiny.

I'll find a way, though the dust is blindin',
I'll take a cloud with a silver linin',
I'll find a land where the sun is always shinin'!
At the end of a dusty road!

Now, I'm sure dozens of lusty baritones have sung that song, singers with far better voices than mine but, I'll venture, never has it been rendered with such heart-rending unction!

But, profitable though it could be, busking was a rarity for me and, as a general rule, I did my Lakeland journey twice between spring and autumn, a slow progression of making a living in my own particular fashion — a rogue and a con-man maybe, but there was in my heart a special affection for the Lake District which has never waned.

11

KNUTTLES OF NAVAN

The origin of jokes is a common topic of conjecture amongst all classes of society. How are they circulated and who invents them? Commercial travellers are blamed for spreading smutty stories, of course, and there can be no doubt that many jokes are based upon true incidents. Tramps were great story-tellers and tales passed on from town to town, from padding-ken to padding-ken, cannibalised or exaggerated, as the case may be.

One of the most popular was the tale of the Yank and the bull, which was attributed to Johnny Knuttles, one of the most outrageous characters on the road in his day. One of his favourite tricks was to tell the time by peering through a bull's back legs. In a certain Yorkshire village, noted for its great beauty and sightseeing excursion buses, Johnny would stand in a field where a bull (a docile one we must assume!) would be keeping its lonely sentinel. When he got a crowd gathered round him he would announce that, for the small sum of one penny per person, he would tell the exact time of the day by looking through the bull's back legs. First of all he would expose his bare arms and empty his pockets in the true professional manner of the Music-Hall conjuror, to prove to the audience that there wasn't a hidden watch on his person. Then after a hocus-pocus of garbled rhetoric he would place his head between the bull's back legs to emerge a few seconds later to announce, 'Twenty-two minutes past three' or whatever the time was. He was always correct, of course, and took a nice collection afterwards. Needless to say this tickled the imagination of the sightseers and the odd foreign tourist. Particularly, a cigar-smoking Yank who was so taken by the display that he offered Knuttles one pound if he would tell him how the trick was performed. The tramp proclaimed that as it was a secret, handed down from generation to generation of the Knuttles family, no amount of money on earth would persuade him to part with the secret. In the end he settled for three pounds ten shillings. Highly delighted, the Yank followed him into the field. Knuttles bade him kneel down alongside him at the bull's rear and both of them placed their heads between the beast's back legs. "Now, sir, this is what you do," said Knuttles quietly. "You move the bull's balls to one side then you can see the clock on the village church."

True or not, it is a typical tramp humour and having travelled with and known the originator it is even possible to believe it.

Not many men can make the claim that they have become a legend in their own lifetime. But one such man was Johnny Knuttles, or Knuttles of Navan as he became known on the road over a period of time in which stories of his exploits became part of the archives of tramp lore, anecdotes to recount around the fire in the padding-ken. For Knuttles was outrageous, rascally, a cheat, con-man, not to be trusted, and thoroughly likeable. The Knuttles stories have been exaggerated so often that it has become almost an impossibility to get to the real truth of the matter but, as I was one of the few men ever to travel with him, I know some of the stories exactly as they happened, yet I have often been sitting at a drum-up along the road, with other tramps, when the subject of Knuttles has come up and the very same stories which I will now recount, and of which I was a witness, were trooped out and grossly misrepresented in the telling. For every tramp was a yarn-spinner by sheer necessity and so the Knuttles legend grew, distorted maybe, but grew just the same to make him one of the most famous tramps on the road. Famous not in the sense W.H. Davies or Jim Phelan are famous, for they are known to the general public through their writings, but Knuttles attained a stature of greatness and respect in vagabondia. A tramp's tramp. Respected because the trait most admired in a tramp's character was the ability to 'take a rise', or to quote a modern Americanism, to 'dupe' John Public. So it is with no little pride that I recount some of the adventures of this tramp-legend because, in some of them, I was his partner.

Knuttles, like most of our ilk, liked to work alone but there were times when he did take a partner if the venture warranted it. An abnormally wet summer had caused me to leave the Lakes earlier than usual and found me in a Sheffield lodging house. He was toasting his bare feet by the fire and casting inquisitive glances at me from the corner of his eye. He could have been weighing me up, suspecting that I was 'carrying' (a rare 'road' word for having money in your pocket), or he could have been a police nark; then again, there was always the possibility he was a homosexual. I challenged him outright, "You wanting something, mate?" The scrawny long neck had the biggest adam's apple it was possible to imagine and it seemed to grow longer like the neck of a rubber man as he gazed hard at me. Then, placing his left hand on his bald head, he slowly brought it down over his eyes and nose in that famous gesture of his, known in the theatre, I am told by those in the know, as the 'slow burn' — a gesture of frustrated agitation.

"Here I am working out how to make a good three week's wages for you and you take me for some cove who's trying to work some dirty trick on you." He even contrived to look hurt.

"I'm sorry, but you were staring at me," I said.

"Of course I was, dear sir. Wouldn't *you* check and double check on the man you are considering taking for a partner?" he asked.

"A partner! What in?"

"Now then, friend," he said, "it is up to you to decide whether you want to hear my proposal or not. I suggest the local boozer across the road, for I am in funds. I think our little discussion will be a three-pint one at the very least. Well, are you game?"

"Three pints each, you must be loaded," I said, impressed.

"I struck an excellent graft today and I don't see any point in setting up in opposition to the Lombard and becoming my own banker, so I spend it," he said with a highly satisfied grin on his ferrety face.

In the pub I was able to get a real look at this character as he stood to his full height in the electric light glow of the 'spit and sawdust' bar. The long neck was but an extension of a long body; an essential feature of every human body, you will say, but in Knuttles's case the body gave the impression of being hardly wider than the neck; a gross exaggeration you will further say and, normally speaking, you will be quite correct, but in his deathless Ulster-type mac the impression was given of continuity in a body without the disruption of a pair of shoulders. The truth was that Nature had provided him with a pair of drastically sloping shoulders to which were attached abnormally long arms and this comical circus-cut of the man was subscribed to by a pair of tall brown boots into which his trousers were unceremoniously stuffed; and a yellow dicky-bow, minus the usual accompanying shirt, responded to every movement of his Adam's apple like a puppet to the play of the puppeteer's fingers.

Such was Knuttles of Navan, one of the best con-men on the road, a man who could milk a 'mark' where a hundred others would fail, and one of the best ghost story (tramp's sob story) tellers ever to disgrace the fair face of England. Now, though Navan is a town in Ireland, Knuttles was not an Irishman. A row with his father precipitated a trip to Ireland at the age of sixteen where he ended up in the town of Navan, staying for a while before he took to the road, tramping round Ireland until he eventually came over to England with three other tramps. The name Knuttles of Navan stuck and so did the impression that he was Irish.

"It's blackberries," he told me in a confessional whisper when we were seated together in a high-backed pew, which made confidential conversation possible. "They're out now, last week in September they're at their best and I reckon we have three weeks. Now you'll be wondering why I've chosen you?"

"The whole thing has me wondering so far," was my answer.

"Then I will proceed to elucidate. You may have noticed that Nature has not provided me with a body one could describe as fat or heavy. In a sentence, I am very fleet of foot despite my fifty years. Now in most padding-kens the men are either too old or too decrepit or just too bone idle to work on the blackberry graft. It's not new, of course, but it always works, or nearly always. You see, when the graft fails (as even the best graft will do sooner or later, friend) then you must take to your heels. How old are you?"

"Thirty-one," I answered.

"Fine. You are youngish and look as fit as a flea to me. You would like to know about the graft?" he queried.

And so I was let into the workings of the Blackberry trick, a simple and easily contrived method of making money but, nevertheless, a successful one. Knuttles was right when he said that it wasn't new, for I have since read Davies's *Super Tramp* in which he tells of the same trick.

So, on the very next morning, I set off with my new partner to put the trick into action. And this is how it worked: having hitch-hiked from the city into the heart of the Derbyshire countryside, we soon found ourselves in bramble-hedged lanes down which it was a delight to walk.

* * * *

There is a magic about September, give me a mild September to a hot July anytime. The honeysuckle was out, twisting and nosing its fragrant way around tree and bush, mingling with the autumnal dun of hedgerow and the redness of haws and rose-hips; and, shining amongst it all, like black jewels in nature's treasure-chest, were the blackberries, wet with dew and glistening like jade in Mother Nature's autumn dress. "Only pick the very best and, whatever you do, don't eat any or you'll get the shits," said Knuttles who had produced some large tins from his pack and we proceeded to pick. After about five minutes he said we had collected quite enough. "Now empty them on the road." He did the same, to produce between us a small pile about enough to make a good-sized pie. He then split the pile into three separate piles. "That lot represents one-and-a-tanner," he announced quite proudly.

"How do you make that out?" I asked. My mentor was too busy to answer.

"Now comes the hard work," he said. "Scour the road,

the hedgerows, or the fields for small stones."

Taking one of the tins, I eventually filled it to the top with stones. He had done the same and so, once more, we emptied the contents onto the road.

"Now," explained Knuttles, "we divide the stones into three — so we'll have three tins each three-quarters full of stones. Now the berries, young Joe, fill each tin to the brim — I think we'll need a few more berries. Only the choicest, now, remember, the fattest juiciest ones possible for the tins must be full to overflowing. We, as tradesmen, have a responsibility to our public. It would never do to be accused of short-measuring them." Knuttles supervised his trickery with the field-science of a general about to implement a military ploy.

When he was satisfied, we carried the tins in our arms — I took two and my partner one. Said Knuttles, "Now, at the end of the lane there's a main road. It carries quite a lot of vehicles and cyclists as well as hikers. They are all possible customers for a giant sixpenny tin of blackberries." Then, as if in a fit of mad ecstasy, he cried, "Look at those lovely hills! There's something about September, young Joe; a sense of tranquillity about the scenery and the atmosphere and where better to stroll than along a Derbyshire lane with those peaks surrounding us like friendly sentinels?" Knuttles loved the countryside, too, and could wax quite lyrical at times about the beauties of nature. But once he had given vent to his thoughts on the softer side of his nature, it was down to business again, a lesson in the methods of blackberry selling. He spoke with authority and the same enthusiasm a scoutmaster has for the instruction he imparts to his troops on knots and making camp fires. "The golden rule is do not call on houses or cottages or the game will be quickly up. What does the housewife do when she gets a tin of blackberries? Why, she wants to give the poor man his tin back, so she empties the fruit into a dish and when she sees she had paid for a pile of stones she is somewhat peeved and runs after the tramp and that spoils his trade and, what's more, the village 'bobby' will be after him and that's the end of the story. No, always sell to a person on the move and give them the tin for good measure, at no extra cost; create the impression that they are getting a bargain — 'Go on, then, keep the tin. I can get another' sort of thing. And above all — keep moving."

Knuttles put his preaching into practice very soon for, approaching in our direction, were a man and woman on hike.

"Good afternoon to you," Knuttles greeted them politely.

After reciprocating the greeting, the woman said: "Oh look! Harry. Blackberries."

"There's plenty along the way," said Harry unimpressed.

"Oh! But these are beauties," said the lady.

"And they took a lot of picking, lady," said Knuttles, with a fine sense of timing. "Feel that, would you." He handed her a tin.

"My! They are big ones — are you selling them?" she asked.

Knuttles pondered. "W . . .ell, I suppose as it would take you a long time to pick as many and seeing as you and the young gent here are on the hike, well . . . right then, I'll sell you a tin for sixpence. A whole hour's picking and sixpence isn't . . ."

"Oh! That's all right," broke in the young chap, anxious to show his lady friend that he wasn't mean. "If you want them, dear, I'll buy them."

"They'll do for tea, Harry."

"Done, and good-day to you, sir, and your lady," said Knuttles.

We repeated the process nine times in all that day, making a total of thirteen shillings and sixpence. Now you might wonder how we obtained the tins, but this was easily done by begging them at houses in the rag and bone-man fashion. With six shillings and ninepence each in our pockets, we arrived in the delightful small town of B- - - - - -. I followed Knuttles along a narrow cobbled lane which skirted the town and was the last man-made creation before the green fields and the hedgerows took over to sweep upwards to the hill which guarded the town from the winds of the East. "Small-town policemen are fussy men," explained Knuttles. "So this lane will conceal us from the gaze of any local constabulary who might be on the beat. What's more, there is a little store on this lane where we will purchase our tea."

After a walk of at least half a mile, we stood before a detached house and I reckoned that we were now on the opposite side of the town from where we had started our circumvention. Knuttles opened the gate and knocked boldly on the door. A tall blonde woman of about forty opened it and immediately she greeted my friend warmly. "Well, Mr Knuttles – – welcome, welcome."

"You have room, Mrs Butterworth?" asked Knuttles.

"For you, Mr Knuttles, certainly . . ."

"And my friend, Joseph, Mrs Butterworth?"

"For a friend of yours, Mr Knuttles, certainly. Come in – – come in, the Major's just arrived."

I was rather surprised to find that the place was a lodging-house, a small one, but still a lodging-house with the kitchen set out in the usual fashion – and the fire. The man she referred to as the Major was sitting by the table, making notes in a diary. "Johnny Knuttles, how are you?" boomed an obviously phoney Oxford accent.

"Blooming, Major, blooming," said Knuttles, shaking hands warmly. "Meet Joseph, a travelling companion."

"Delighted, Joseph." The Major slapped me heartily on the back. From the shabby tweed suit down to his battered brogues, taking into account the florid beery face, with the waxed moustache, I judged the man a phoney. If he was a major then I was the Emperor of Mesopotamia. I had met lots of genuine ex-military men and he didn't fill the bill. "We're just in time for compers, aren't we Mrs B? That's the stuff."

Whilst Mrs B. went off to bring in the complimentary tea, Knuttles and the Major smiled knowingly at one another and then each eased the boots from his weary feet. That smile spoke volumes which words could not have conveyed. It was the heart-music of two rogues in close harmony, for each knew that the other was a cheat and that both, for years, had been playing up to the image the class conscious Mrs Butterworth expected them to keep up. For this was a residence for travelling men, not a common lodging-house, so Mrs B. Maintained. It was one grade up from the run-of-the-mill establishments to be found in every town, but a lodging-house for tramps just the same. She liked to pick and choose her 'clients' and had put up her rates accordingly, so that she supposed she was attracting a better class of man. In actual fact she attracted a better class of con-man. Or, to be more correct, a higher grade, for a man had to have good 'marks' to be able to afford to stop in the place for a night. Not that Mrs B. would ever admit she catered for tramps, she gave the impression of living in a make-believe world as she hung on to every word the Major said and made it obvious in her own conversation that she didn't let 'anybody' stay; in a sentence, she tried to attract the man down on his luck, who had known better days and who spoke with an educated accent rather than the old grey tramp who called a spade a spade and would much prefer a 'real' doss-house anyway. You could never have boiled your hosiery along with your spuds in Mrs B's. And that would never have done for many men I knew.

The Major was typical of her guests. She boasted doctors, army officers, bankers and professors amongst her clients; some were genuinely from 'How the mighty are fallen' brigade, men struck off the professional register for misdemeanours. Others were completely bogus but gifted by nature with the ability to act. And the Major, who's real name was plain Jack Grice and not Major Parsons, was a good example of the latter type — charming, full of vocal blandishments, with a repertoire of disarming guile that would get him a box-seat at a heavenly concert. And he had a great way with the women. He had served five years in Walton for fraud and had conned his way round Ireland during the World War to keep out of the way of the recruiting drives. All this Knuttles told me later. There is, of course, a 'major' in every doss-house and in every pub. Ask 'has the Major been in' and you will be told that he is in, has been in or will be coming in.

The most alluring feature of the house was the luxury of heated bedrooms; there were two, each with a fire made and fed with twigs and pieces of branches collected from the woods. Winter and summer there was always a fire and so, in the winter, Mrs Butterworth's became a very popular establishment. Besides, she changed the sheets twice a week and 'shuffled' the blankets daily so, if you were staying for a few days, you never got the same blanket twice. So naturally enough, bugs were passed on from occupant to occupant although one was never as conscious of it as in other houses and of course these were of a superior breed needless to say! The complimentary tea was one of her little touches to add to the effect of shabby gentility and an excuse to put an extra penny on the charge. For like the Major and the rest of her clients, she was a phoney, a hard-headed business woman inside her floral apron and outward expression of middle-class respectability.

"Ah! Compers," said the Major when the tea-pot arrived. "Not every house you get complimentary afternoon tea, Mrs B., you know," he fawned.

Mrs B. beamed at the Major. "Well, you know I like to do things correctly, Major. And I know my Gentlemen appreciate these little touches of gentility to which they are accustomed."

"We do indeed," said the Major, oozing unction, but as soon as she had gone from the room, he said, "If the old bag calls this muck tea then my name's Tommy Lipton. It will have to have its usual five minutes stir. She buys the sweepings up from the tea warehouses when she goes into Manchester — oh! here's some of the other boys arriving." And as the house gradually filled up it was obvious to me that these men were all of a similar type to the Major, the 'Top Cocks' of the road who went in for the more profitable marks, relying on their ability to act and tell a good story for a large return. The most common class of tramp was the man who walked only a very few miles each day, contrary to the supposition that tramps walk long distances each day. He had to make his living like any other man and to a tramp that meant having something for the pan at the end of the day — for a man who had nothing was despised as a mug. But the long-distance men like these men were known as postmen, not the letter-delivering species, but tramps who had one, or sometimes two, pre-destined calls in mind for the day and so they set aside all the temptations to catch the smaller fry, preferring to go after the big fish. Clergymen, retired Army Colonels and philanthropic business men were the main targets of the postman's long journeying.

I have never been a postman, much preferring to keep to

one circuit, travelling it year in, year out. A comparison of the difference between myself and a postman can be struck by citing the example of the commercial traveller who calls on every small back-street grocery shop in the big city as opposed to the man who calls on the big wholesale accounts which are spread wide apart.

I had my best meal for years that evening, dining on a pork chop with a tent-peg (egg) and a packet of biscuits washed down by a pot of really good quality tea of the type rarely used by a tramp. This was topped off by two bottles of pale ale and a cheroot. I enjoyed that evening, a full belly and the knowledge that a heated bedroom awaited me, plus the assurance from Knuttles that our financial success could be repeated many times, as long as the blackberries lasted. And what an educational few hours I spent as I listened to the fireside tales for, as they were nearly all postmen, there was no need for the usual 'Council of Commerce' – a nightly ritual in doss-houses when the tramps decide who shall travel on which road and in which direction. It is no use ten tramps in one day calling at the same house, but the postman is a law unto himself, a true professional and the top of the tramping tree. So the talk was of the men's adventures; the 'fast ones' worked on a gullible public, and it ended with a most enlightening and entertaining mini-lecture from the Major on how to deal with Military Officer-Gentlemen and the art of relieving them of their money. His technique was to study the history of the regiment of the old soldier he was to call on so that by the time he called on the old boy he would be fully conversant with the regiment's campaigns, successes in battle, its heroes and its Generals. He specialised in ex-cavalrymen.

"Once rode a horse, so it comes natural," he explained. "But these old buffers aren't idiots, you know. They won't tolerate Privates who come the sob story, there's too many of them about. But I go as one of themselves. I mean, for all they know, I might have ridden next to them at Balaclava, I'm of their own type, don't you know. Seen better days, you know; a Gentleman down on his luck, might be the horses or the drink or a fondness for the flossies – they've all been men of the world, you know, and a Gentleman doesn't pry into the unfortunate circumstances of another.

'Damned dodgy the Stock Exchange at the moment' one old dodderer said to me only yesterday and I agreed. He assumed I'd lost everything in Consolidated Tungsten so I didn't contradict him. You see, it's the impression you create, let them form their own opinions, then they give me a little loan for the sake of the old regiment and old times. But they have a sharp eye, you know; must look the part. Saddle sore and slightly bandy, that's the rule."

To be with tramps who had money to spare was a unique experience and I knew that I was an interloper amongst the élite of the profession. And as the beer warmed the nostalgia which is present in the heart of every tramp, even the flamboyant Major Parsons had to give way by popular demand to Knuttles, who was called upon to tell us of his celebrated adventures.

"Tell us about the boots, Johnny," prompted the tramp known as the 'professor'.

"I'm due for a new pair shortly, sure enough," laughed Knuttles, glancing down at his down-at-heel footwear. "Well, it's like this," he began, "and I don't know why more of you don't do the same thing. Mind you, it's all in the way you do it, do it with self-assurance and a bucketful of cheek and you'll get away with it, don't you agree, Major?"

"The essence of the trade," agreed the bogus old campaigner with a self-assured chuckle.

"Well I work the Lewis's circuit mainly — Liverpool, Manchester and Leeds — never do the same store twice, if you can help it. There's an old saying that 'Fair exchange is no robbery'. I'm not sure that being 'fair' is part of my technique, but it works just the same. When Christmas is over and the January sales begin that's the time — a heaven-sent opportunity. The time of the year when folks go beserk after bargains. Rugby scrums have nothing on the scrimmages of humanity fighting over the cheap lines. I make for the Gents' Shoe Dept. And after a lot of pushing and shoving I work my way gradually to the counter where all the sale's lines are on display. Now in the mêlée nobody notices what the next man is doing, being too intent on his own business — that of buying a pair of shoes or boots at the cheapest price possible before someone else beats you to it. So with all the aplomb I can muster, I simply kick off my own shoddy footwear until I am standing in my stockinged feet. Then, having chosen a pair of boots of the right size for my feet, I try them on and as I am doing so, hustling, bustling and bending, along with the rest of the bargain hunters, I place my old pair on the counter amongst the rest of the shoes. A simple case of exchange, you see. Then, in a loud voice, bemoaning the fact that the store hasn't a pair to fit my feet, I make my disgruntled way outside, leaving them to it. I do it every year and hope to be able to do it when the January sales come round again."

One of the postmen roared with laughter when the tale was finished, but the Major silenced him by holding up his hand. "Gentlemen," he said, "what you have just heard is an account of a stroke of genius. And would any store take action against the man if he was caught? No, why to be conned in such a fashion is a privilege!"

And then we all burst into the biggest belly-laugh chorus ever heard in Mrs Butterworth's kitchen. There was so much noise she came in to investigate the cause of the merriment.

"Just Mr Knuttles telling us some of his stories, Mrs B.," explained the Major in his oily way. "I do hope we are not keeping you from your well-earned slumber, my dear."

"Oh! No, not at all, Major. Simply curious. Well, I'll leave you to it, knowing what you gentlemen of the world are like, I suppose some of the stories are not for a lady's ears. Men will be men, hey Major?"

"But not with you, you old bag," said Major when Mrs B. had left us. "Never did fancy the woman. Can't tolerate women with dyed yellow hair. Well, how about another whip-round for a jug of ale? Here, you're the youngest, laddy," turning to me. "We'll give you the honour of going for the supper beer."

I scooped up the small change from the table then picked up the large water jug to take to the local pub.

"You will come back, old boy, won't you?" said the Major with a leer.

"If you'd sooner someone else go, then here's the money," I replied, making it quite obvious that I didn't care for his insinuation.

"No offence, old chap. Simply my little joke, don't you know."

There was something so sickeningly false about the man that I felt like wiping the grin off his face. I was used to chicanery and deception, for it is the stock-in-trade of the tramp, but there is honour even amongst thieves but I wouldn't have trusted our bogus Major even if he had sworn on a stack of Bibles. And I hadn't missed the look on his face when the 'professor' had inadvertently let a pound note drop onto the table whilst he was rooting for coppers for the whip-round. Knuttles saw the note, too, and so had 'Johnny the one' — another of the set — who had the shiftiest eyes I had ever seen in a man. I had a premonition that the 'professor's' paper currency might soon be in a state of fluctuation.

When I returned with the beer, 'Johnny the one' emptied a half-full medicine bottle containing Methylated Spirits into the jug and gave it a stir with a large pudding spoon. I knew enough about the ways of the road to be aware that such a mixture acts like an anaesthetic on a man and I purposely refused to drink any, making myself some tea instead. I wanted to be sufficiently sober to be alerted if there was any movement during the night.

12

MORE WAYS OF MAKING A LIVING

Early the next morning I awoke to the sound of pouring rain and it wasn't to cease for four whole days, washing away the blackberry bonanza with a torrential disregard for the pounds, shillings and pence of a couple of tramp-rogues. And then I was alerted by the unmistakable sound of boot steel scraping on a wooden floor. Ears sharpened to nocturnal sounds interpreted the movements as activity that was up to no good. An act of light-fingered work was about to be carried out and this was a time to count one's possessions. My clothes were under the pillow, my boots pinioned to the floor by the bed legs. This was a trick I learned the hard way, for in my early days I had a pair of boots stolen in Salisbury House in St. Helens. I suddenly remembered the 'Prof's' pound note, several pairs of eyes had seen that slip of his, and none more avariciously than those of Johnny the One, a scoundrel if I ever saw one. Furthermore, whoever it was had slept in his boots, and I distinctly recalled Johnny's rough-shod boots. A shaft of anaemic moonlight silhouetted a man's form. There was a rustle, a flick as of a thumb and forefinger fingering a note. Cautious tip-toed steps picked their way to the door and then the stairs creaked slightly, but ever so slightly for this was an accomplished thimble-rigger (pickpocket) at work. I followed in my bare feet. The fire had gone out and the sound of snoring testified to the anaesthetic potency of the methylated punch. And Johnny the One had put the spirit in the beer. I followed down the stairs, across the kitchen and out into the wet night. It was essential for me to discover the culprit, for I knew that some of these veteran roadsters secretly considered me a 'young mug'. I had given up looking for permanent work long since, but they didn't know this and so if the pound was stolen I would be the suspect. And I was a stranger, even to Knuttles almost. Through the murk I could see my man pulling on a coat. This was my chance for his arms were momentarily held by the sleeves and so he couldn't resist and I had him fast by the jacket lapels. The bogus Major Parsons glared at me with terror in his eyes.

"The pound, Major," I said quietly. There was no hesitancy and the note crinkled in my palm and, like a beaten dog, he slunk away into the night, knowing he was fortunate to escape without a thrashing.

Now in that year of little, 1930, a pound note represented considerable wealth. Many a man would have slaved at any job for a week just to take it home in order to feed his kids and stop them begging for bread in the street. I suddenly realised that I had never actually possessed a whole pound note before, not to call my own. It represented clothes and a new pair of boots, even the chance of a job; ten years previous I might have pocketed the note, but I was a tramp now — and I didn't want to keep it, a strange anomaly. But any temptation I had was squashed by the rain, and Mrs B's kip-room was warm. The incident went completely unnoticed for the 'professor' still had his note when he awoke and everyone assumed that the major's early departure had been precipitated by a wish to reach one of his military suckers early in the day. I kept my lips buttoned tight over the incident, but three years later the major wasn't so fortunate, for he was found dead in a doss-house kitchen. His murderer was never found and if anyone knew the truth then this was a secret that was never revealed on the tramp grapevine.

That morning me and Johnny Knuttles began a journey of pointless wandering, a couple of drowned gutter-dogs getting wetter and more disenchanted with our lot by the hour. Our clothes were saturated, our boots leaking like colanders and that peculiar type of cold caused by excessive wetting turning our limbs to heavy unfunctionable lumps, leaden and throbbing. Rain, next to cold, was the tramp's arch enemy, and we were having a taste of both at once, and for four days we plodded on, telling the tale at houses for cups of tea and bread, chopping wood and drying our clothes after a fashion in the doss-house kitchen, and the next morning we wore them again, sodden smelling rags.

"Verily, Joseph, we need new togs," said Knuttles in the psuedo-Shakesperian manner he loved to use.

We had progressed to Derby by this time, the fourth day of the great deluge and were standing outside a large Gents' outfitters. A sale was in progress. We wandered in and Knuttles nonchalantly unhooked an overcoat from a stand and put it on. It would have fitted both of us, but Johnny didn't worry about sizes. He took another and this went on top of the first one and then he made for the door, leisurely, as unconcerned as if he had paid cash on the nail. When he reached the door I followed. But he had been spotted. Eager youth in the shape of a gangling lad in a pin-stripe staff issue suit was questioning him: "Where are you going, sir?"

"To the window to try it in the light."

"But you have *two* coats on, sir."

"You invite selection, don't you, young man?" said Knuttles sharply. "Well, I don't like either of them," and, peeling them off, he flung them over the outstretched arm of the salesman and out we walked into the street.

"If you want to get inside for a rest I'd try chucking a brick through a jeweller's window," I said. The mention of prison annoyed him, for it was his proud boast that he had never been inside one. Pride in his ability to commit the perfect petty larceny was stronger than any desire to be warm and well fed in a prison cell.

The next day the rain stopped only to be replaced by fog and we were into what was to be one of the worst Octobers on record. Knuttles 'told the tale' in the manner born. There was no holding back with Johnny, simply walking up to a door and asking to see the owner of the house. Our rigmarole of bluff and recitals of dire misfortune became part of our way of life and, once into the swing of the business, it became almost a pleasure. A vocal examination with the prize for a pass being a bowl of soup, or a thick hunk of bread and cheese, sometimes money and often as much tea as it was possible to drink. Knuttles disregarded the 'please wet my tea, missus' routine. He was a man buffeted by life's tempests, vomited forth from the volcanoes of desperately bad luck and, like stupid fish grabbing at worms, they swallowed the lot.

One frosty morning at a small house near Warrington, we decided to offer our services as woodcutters. We had been told by a chap on his way from a casual ward that the woman had once paid him handsomely for the job. She greeted us favourably enough when Knuttles said, "We'd like to earn a shilling, marm, cutting firewood, the weather being so cold for you."

"Come round the back," she said, plainly pleased by the offer.

Before us, in the yard, was a mountain of timber. It would have taken four men with double-handed saws to do the job.

"If you cut that lot up I'll give you sixpence apiece and a bowl of good thick soup."

"Blimey, marm, I asked you to let us earn a shilling not keep us in work for life!" said Knuttles in disgust.

"Ugh! Too lazy are you, like the rest of them. Bone idle that's your trouble," and she ordered us to leave immediately or she'd have the police on us.

In Wigan Knuttles spotted a pie cooling on a wooden seat outside a cottage window. The sight of its curling steam nearly sent me mad with hunger.

"Go and sit across the road," ordered the director of operations. By this time we were really ragged, the rain had twisted and wrung our clothing into grotesque shapes, mud-caked as if it had been spread by a plasterer's trowel. A young woman crossed the road to avoid me when I sat down on a bench opposite the cottage. And yet there were hundreds of men in Wigan dressed like me. They weren't tramps, simply jobless men begging for food and brawling on slag heaps searching for pieces of coal. Perhaps she didn't know about them.

Knuttles was returning down the path with the steaming pie. The woman's eyes blazed. "You've stolen that," she twittered in amazement.

"Stolen, madam! Certainly not," said Knuttles. We had a spoon apiece in our sacks, which we had 'forgotten' to leave behind in the doss-house at Leigh and we delved into the pie, not knowing or caring what was inside. It was potato and onion and delicious. The young woman had gathered reinforcements, namely the woman of the cottage and her husband. The trio charged at us across the lane but Johnny halted them in their tracks when he said "Thanks, missus, the pie is delicious. What a wonderful Christian thought to put food out for two men who are out of work. We will call at the priest's house to tell him of your kindness. Mrs . . .?"

"Hill — Freda Hill," said the pie-maker without thinking.

"Eat up, Joe. Mrs Hill wants the plate back," said Johnny digging into a large piece of crust.

The husband nearly choked on his indignation and the two women were stuck for words.

"Yes, we won't forget this," continued Knuttles thickly, crunching greedily. "The priest will know about this immediately we've finished. It's the least we can do, Mrs Hill. Not many would do what you've done and I'll make sure he knows it. You're a real Christian Mrs Hill. My friend Joe, here, would thank you too, only he can't speak, poor lad."

"Why, what's matter wit' lad?" asked Mr Hill.

"Throat, can't speak. It's all this rain, hot drinks might help, but then we've no means . . ."

"What's tha waiting for, Freda lass? Can't see as't lad's poorly, put t'kettle on t'hob lass. Come on, bring t'pie wi' thee and sit thee by t'fire."

Before the fire in the kitchen we finished off that magnificent pie which was helped down by mugs of tea, while Knuttles told the most remarkable tale yet. We had, said Knuttles, been sacked from the coalmines for helping the families of the strikers. Immediately we were on home ground for Mr Hill was a retired collier and he warmed to our plight.

"Lousy sods them colliery owners. Wouldn't part wi' their own muck, not them sods."

And then, continued Knuttles, we had slept rough whilst we searched for work along the length and breadth of the country until, one day, unable to keep awake, we had committed the cardinal sin of sleeping in a public library. The police were called and we were thrown out into the rain. Not a hand-out or a roof over our head had we had for four days, until we had had our steps directed to the kind woman who put food outside for starving men – –. Mrs Hill was crying. To think she had actually meant to eat that pie herself! Her husband was making queer sounds, too. His belly was rumbling. We had eaten his dinner and yet he was so touched by the sob-story he was glad to forfeit it to two honest God-fearing men, good Catholics to boot, on the breadline. And when Knuttles suggested we kneel down together to say a **prayer of thanks-giving to God, the Hills felt quite charit**able. By doing unto us they had done unto Him. Charity had been thrust upon them. We said the 'Our Father . . . and Knuttles gave the amen to it by invoking God to bless the house. If the pair of us had been struck down by the Almighty Lord we couldn't have grumbled. I felt uncomfortable surrounded by all the holy pictures on the wall of the kitchen. The old couple were good Samaritans and yet almost on the breadline themselves: that cottage floor was pitted by subsidence, for a lot of property in the Wigan area had been built on coalmines; damp walls bore patches of green fungus. And I had stolen their dinner! I had despised the major for what he had done, but here was I sponging off an old couple who had fallen for a pack of lies but who gave because they were poor. They knew the feeling of hunger and despair. They were the poor of the land and, like all the poor, they gave to the poor. This was the most startling lesson I learned on the road. The kindred spirit between those who were down, no matter how low, shone bright and never more **fervently** than when those even lower down the scale of life were starving. I found that no matter how poor a family was they could always spare something for the tramp. The more fortunate ones and the rich could be kind, too, but they could never be depended upon. They gave as caprice took them, and a tramp couldn't live on sheer chance; so when he was desperate he went to the poor. They understood. Many people gave on conditions. They pried, made propositions, used bribery to work on the emptiness of a stomach. But the poor didn't quiz, they simply gave. Jack London, the tramp-author summed up charity when he said 'A bone to the dog is not charity. Charity is the bone shared with the dog when you are just as hungry as the dog'. The tramp was the dog, the low cur of society, the word signified lowliness. And never did I feel lower than when tucking into what was probably the only food the old couple had in the house. The fact that I had cheated churches of money from the Sunday collections didn't worry me, neither did any other trickery I had practised, there was no hardship inflicted by my cozenage and deceit. But now I felt I was spitting in the eye of true charity.

Our farewells said, we set off with a string of blessings ringing in our ears. Knuttles anticipated my outburst. Knuttles always knew, the fellow was an amazing student of human nature. He stopped me in my first sentence.

"You think I'm a swine, Joe. O.K. right enough, to take the food from a nice old couple like them is unforgivable. But you see, Joe, the art of the deception is **dependent** upon strategy. Take the pie . . ."

"You did take the pie!" I broke in scornfully.

"Exactly. And you enjoyed it, too."

"It's stuck in my throat. I'd vomit it back only my guts are too hungry to part with it."

"Quite so. You see, you are agreeing with me, Joe. Strategy. Planning. Spur-of-the-moment decision making. The very essence of survival on the road, Joseph. You see, the good story is the key to success in obtaining food, so in the case of the pie I knew instinctively that I would have to have an answer ready. An answer so spontaneous, so breathtakingly outrageous that recrimination was out of the question. The old couple took us in – – –"

"I would have said *we* took the old couple in . . ." I broke in again. Sarcasm hung on every syllable, but Johnny didn't worry.

"You see," he continued "the tramp must size up his victim. Two good **Catholics**, so I mentioned the priest. Catholics adore the priest you see, he is the Father-figure, they fear him really. To offer praise from him to a poor parishioner is bait – good bait."

"But how did you know they were Catholics?" I wanted to know.

"I didn't. The best laid plan will often fail if one doesn't take a chance. Besides, if they had been Methodists the word 'priest' is not far removed from parson or preacher or, say, vicar. Now, the fact remains that they are Catholics and if I am not mistaken there, ahead of us, is the Catholic Church. Let us see if we can get the priest to open his larder." And without more ado Knuttles strode up the path leading to the priest's house and I dallied at a distance, nervous about what was going to happen next.

A typical Irish housekeeper opened the door. "Well, what is it?" The bulldog snap in her voice and manner let us know she knew a tramp when she saw one and was nobody's fool. Priests and parsons were the continual prey of tramps.

"We want to see Father Gilpin, please," said Knuttles politely. Mrs Hill had told us his name and this was a new tramp-approach judging by the look on the woman's face.

"Oh, you know him do you?"

"Let us say we know of him. We come on behalf of one of his parishioners."

"Oh! Indeed now do ye?" Lines of suspicion spread across her face. "Then ye'll wait here."

We heard a bell ring. Minutes later an elderly, grey-haired priest came to the door. "Who are you?" he asked.

Knuttles answered: "Mrs Hill's brother — Freda Hill up the road at the cottages. I've come to tell you she's in a poor state, Father."

"And judging by the pair of you, you don't seem to have come from the land of plenty yourselves. Come in, would you." The housekeeper was still suspicious and obviously the boss.

"They'll not sit on the chairs in your study in those clothes, Father. If they come in it's here they'll stay or out they'll go."

"Miss O'Riordan is plagued by tramps, you know, and she's after thinkin' as you're the same."

Miss O'Riordan went "Ugh!" The priest sat us down at an ancient table in the kitchen and told the woman to make us tea.

"Before you tell me what it is you've come about, I'll make a phone call," said the priest.

"New fangled toy – uses it at every chance. More waste of money." The housekeeper was mumbling and kept casting contemptuous glances at us. Knuttles's eyes and one of his long bony arms strayed to a shelf on which were several wine bottles. "You needn't look at them, they're all dead," snapped Miss O'Riordan.

"But I'll bet they didn't die without the priest," said Knuttles quick as a flash.

"Now then, let's hear what ye've to tell me," said the priest when he sat at the table, whilst the housekeeper set out the crockery. Fr. Gilpin was a good listener and never said a word during Knuttles's ghost story (Lying tale).

"I'm Freda's young brother, Thomas. Mind you, you'd hardly recognise any resemblance, Father, for these last years I've lived from hand to mouth, fighting the drink. Well, you see, Father, I was the black sheep of the family. Ten there were and I was the family rotter. Brought shame on them I did – drink, women and betting. I don't need to tell you, Father, how these evils can drag a man down. But you see, if a lad's had a good upbringing then there's always a chance. My poor old mother was Godfearing and, Father, I can remember how she prayed for me – often as not when the rest of them were on their knees I was out at the pub or lying on my bed in a drunken stupor. Not one brass farthing did I give her, Father, and poor old daddy was a sick man. Consumption. Slaved in the pits with hardly a thank you at the end of it. Ten mouths to feed. They were desperate days, Father, though times are bad enough now. Well, I abused them, the mother and father who were kindness itself. When I think of her now I'm overcome with grief. Oh! I'm so ashamed, Father, that I can't get her face out of my mind – lined with worry and hard work, an old woman twenty years before her time with a son who whored – begging your pardon, madam (this to the housekeeper who was unashamedly wiping the tears from her eyes with a handkerchief) and boozed every penny he could lay his hands on. I stole from her, Father – God help me, but I stole from my own mother. And then daddy died — a terrible lingering death he had, Father — and I left home, despised by my brothers and sisters, or so I thought, Father, so I thought. But, as I told you, that good Catholic upbringing was with me all the time. Never could I shake off the feeling that someone was with me. And, Father, I know deep in my heart of hearts that those parents of mine were battering at the gates of Heaven — from the inside, of course, Father — to make Almighty God listen and have mercy on their poor wandering, pitiful son who had brought so much anguish into their lives. For you see, Father, it's never too late and that fine example they gave me gradually gave me the lift I needed. I fought back. It was hard — brutally hard — but gradually I pulled myself up, gave up the drink. I married a fine girl. Oh! She was a girl my poor old mother would have been proud of, Father, but she died in childbirth. I was hit hard. I couldn't take it. I was demoralised. Back again I went to the bottle; harder and harder I hit it — befuddled with drink I fought with the foreman. I got the sack and I was on the streets. Years I roamed like a tramp, Father. I knew the whereabouts of only one of my family, Freda. God forgive me for ever doubting she could be charitable to her swine of a brother, begging your pardon again, marm (again to the sniffing Miss O'Riordan) and so I never did look her up. And so the years went and again I got the chance of a job. Again I fought back and do you know, Father, the power of prayer of the Holy Souls in Heaven must be able to move mountains. I gave up the drink again, found work and lived in lodgings. Each day was a titanic struggle against the call of the bottle but I did it. Back I went to my duties, Father. All those years away from Church, but back I went — God bless that mother of mine — and then the steelworks closed. I was out of work like many thousands of men. On the streets again I met Joseph here — another Catholic by the way, Father — and Joe and me have been battering at doors asking for work, queueing in the early hours of the morning for anything to earn a few shillings. And then we found ourselves in Wigan, Father. I remembered Freda. She greeted me for what I was, her long lost brother, the prodigal son of the Bible returning home, his past sins forgotten. She fed us, Father, gave us the food she had prepared for herself and her husband. She's a good sort and I'm worried about her. You see, me and Joe here well we're on our way looking for work, walking through the night to Birmingham where, we're told, there's the chance of a job. She's got no food left, she wouldn't admit it so I'm asking you, Father, to see they get some food. Could you send them up something? Only don't say I've called, Father. She wouldn't like it if she knew I'd been to see you."

Even Father Gilpin had to have a good hard blow in his handkerchief as Knuttles came to the end of his harrowing narrative. "God bless you for an open and honest confession. It does you great credit to show concern for your sister. Miss O'Riordan here will take her some food: it sounds serious."

"Indeed I will, Father — I'll see to it right away, sure I will. But, Father Gilpin, what about these poor men's clothes? Sure they're not fit to be on scarecrows in the field."

"It's taken care of, Miss O'Riordan. That new fangled toy you're always chastising me for using and running up bills has been useful. The Misses O'Gorman will fit them both out with clothes. I'll give you a note . . . Now, before you go up to the Hills, Miss O'Riordan, would you ever make some more tea and bring the loaf and the homemade jam you're hidin' in the cupboard and the slab cake. I think we'll all have an early tea."

Full of homemade bread and blackberry jam and armed with the letter to the Mesdames O'Gorman, we set off to a big house in the country where the women lived. The clothes transformed us from obvious tramps into working men. Johnny proposed we went in for a spell of griddling; he would do the singing and I would act as the collector. I agreed as long as he didn't expect me to sing. I still had pride and I was adamant in not using my voice for gutter wailing. Knuttles had a voice broken in many a doss-house cats' concert, but more than that he had the right approach to the business. The most maggoty tramp thought all he had to do was start singing and the coppers would rattle in the tin, but

Knuttles knew that the secret of successful griddling was to create the impression that you were a respectable man down on your luck — fate had dealt you a hard blow and there you were forced to sing for pennies in the street. Dishevelled but decent that was the secret of the successful griddler. In our second-hand charity hand-me-downs we fitted the bill, each day spent on the pad adding to the appearance of decrepit decency which John Public found so appealing. 'There but for the grace of God go I' was the emotion created and we spent several weeks at the game, making our way slowly from town to town on no particular route. My job was to go round with the tin while Knuttles griddled or, when we were working the houses, he would stand in the middle of the road chanting while I knocked on the doors. In a highly respectable neighbourhood in Southport my friend's dreadful tonsorial rendering was offending the ears of the residents, but as he was in the road and I was collecting from house to house, it was I who received a full chamberpot of water over my head. A few houses further up the road I was lucky not to be savaged by an Alsation as I stood in the garden. As the brute leapt at me a stern voice commanded it to 'stay!' "Now then, beggarman, let that be a lesson to you," said its owner. "Next time I'll turn him on you properly." Tenacity of purpose had to be a strong point in my make-up so I still persevered, collecting the odd sixpence but mostly pennies and half-pennies, many a resounding expletive and plenty of threats to set the dog on me or call a policeman. And all the time Knuttles droned away like a set of leaking bagpipes, unconcerned that the dangerous part of griddling was asking for money.

In Liverpool we were arrested and put in a cell for the night, but let off with a caution at the Petty Sessions on the next day. So many men were on the streets singing and begging during the slump of the Thirties that to have sent the lot to prison would have overtaxed the prison service. Knuttles's one and only song was a sordid dirge of an Irish folk song called "The louse house in Kilkenny", the story of Buck Singen's notorious lodging establishment where Knuttles claimed he had once had the misfortune to stay during his Irish travels. The song nauseated me, not alone by its words, but by his continual repetition of it. I tried to teach him the words of more melodious songs with more appeal, but he only knew the one song and said it was the best a griddler could sing, its beauty being its touching refrain. But, in my view, the words are enough to make the flesh creep.

> Oh! The first of me downfall,
> I set out the door
> I straight me way on Concarrickon's shore.
> Going out by Rathrouen t'was late in the night
> Going out the Westgate to view the gaslight.
>
> Chorus
>
> With me Fol - - di - - de - - diddle idad de diddle deeoh!
>
> I went to the tonsil to see the big lamp
> And who should I meet but a bloody big tramp.
> I kindly stepped over and to him I said,
> "Would you kindly direct me to where I'll get a bed."
>
> Chorus
>
> Twas then he directed me down to Cook's Lane.
> To where old Buck Singen kept an old sleeping cage.
> Hung out on the door was a small piece of board.
> Hung out on two nails was a small piece of cord.
>
> Chorus
>
> Well I looked up and down till I found out the door
> And a queer-looking household I n'er saw before
> Then the Missies came out and these words to me said,
> "If you give me three coppers I'll give you a bed."
>
> Chorus
>
> Well I then stood aside with me back to the wall.
> And the next thing I saw was an old cobbler's stall.
> And there was the cobbler and he mended his brogues

> With his hammers and pitchers all laid in a roll.
>
> *Chorus*
>
> Then she brought me upstairs and she put out the light
> And in less than five minutes I had to show fight
> And in less than five more when the story was let
> The fleas came around me and brought me a curse.
>
> *Chorus*
>
> Twas all round me body they formed a march
> Twas all round me body they played the dead march
> But the bloody old Major gave me such a pick
> That he nearly made way with the half of me hip!
>
> *Chorus*
>
> Now I'm agoing to me study these words to pen down
> And if any poor traveller should e'er come to town
> If any poor traveller benighted like me
> Beware of Buck Singen and his Black Calvary.
>
> *Chorus*

As I still persisted in not allowing my stupid pride to let me sing, Knuttles sang it day after day, on streets, markets, outside football grounds and any time we happened to come across people gathered together. Though I didn't care for the job, I had to agree that we made a fair living.

Our tour took us to Manchester where it was so cold some days we sat for hours on end in sleazy cafes warming our hands on mugs of tea and trying to make them last as long as possible. Bloody Mary's was still in business and such was the stability of prices in those days that a night's dossing cost sixpence, the same price I had paid over ten years before. Human wrecks frequented the back street cafes, meths drinkers scrounged and begged in Piccadilly and, as the light faded, the prostitutes and the pimps took over on the street corners, in doorways, and outside the pubs; tawdry tarts with painted faces like witches staring into the eyes of passing men. The Woodbine hanging from the lips was the moonshine of their calling, always accompanied by a request for a match. As we slouched along we had time to study the faces of the women; who were they, why were they on the game? Had they once been respectable women? Our appearance probably aroused the same thoughts in their minds. Like tramps, they came from various backgrounds. One I met in a pub was brought up in a convent, another was a vicar's daughter. Some of them were very pretty girls, but the bloom of beauty was a short-lived one for the oldest profession was a hard taskmaster and these women grew old and haggard long before their time. For they lived like machines and, like them, became worn out; the old dyed-haired harridans of the street were pitiful to see, harlots who still went out hoping some desperate, equally pitiful man, would reward them with the price of some supper. But it was seldom indeed that even these old crones would look on a tramp as a potential customer. That's how low he was. As I think back now I realise that the hardest blow of all to a man at tramp level must be this complete contempt for him shown by the female sex. With women he has no chance. The feeling is one of demoralisation, castration of spirit, self-abasement that shatters man's pride on the rocks of despair. A woman can show pity and exhibit understanding but of his manhood she is contemptuous.

All-night tea-stalls were the haunts of the night people. Rather than spend a few coppers on a bed they would stay until the early hour of next morning standing at tea counters, sipping half-penny cups of tea and hoping to be treated by some late-night revellers on their way home from a party or the theatre. It is interesting to note that, with the average working wage at £2 in 1930, the cost of living left little over for Bacchanalian delights. Such everyday commodities as fags (Woodbines) were 4d for a packet of ten; the larger ones, such as Player's and Senior Service (definitely the middle-class smokes) 6d for ten; common mild ale was 3½d a pint, whilst the services of a prostitute cost on the average half-a-crown. Fish and chips was the staple diet of tens of thousands of folk and a little luxury at 1½d a bagful when I was in funds.

Street fighting was common, mostly outside pubs at throwing out time but not unusual at any time for men with nothing else to occupy themselves, yet it was safe to walk the streets at night, old ladies never gave it a second thought and policemen were seven feet tall — or so it seemed. The mugger, the flick-knife and the bicycle chain were still the property of movie hoodlums. In my days on the streets the man out for trouble picked someone his own size. The colliers loved brawling and, next to Irish navvies, were the hardest bunch of men in the country. To walk by night through a large city is an education, for one is faced by a world that the man who sleeps in his bed never knows. A city never sleeps. It has a voice and its sounds are different from its daytime symphony of hustle and bustle, but it still speaks in a language that the night-dweller understands; to him it holds no fear for he is a citizen of the dark; like so many mice crawling from their hidey-holes, the Cimmerian folk brought the city alive when it should have been dead, people who were frightened of daylight, those upon whom the sun never shone. They were the most pitiable of life's failures and yet they were often people with personalities and eccentricities that respectable society missed, covering the whole kaleidoscope of human character.

We had walked through the heart of the city, not having the price of a kip between us but enough for a cup of soup and a crust of bread apiece, which we had put off until three o'clock in the morning, trying to sleep in doorways and smothering ourselves in old newspapers on park benches. At the tea stall we met a man who obviously liked taking a rise out of the other customers. Judging by his supercilious air and one-time Savile Row suit, stained and shining with over wear and an attempt to 'hot-iron' it back to its former elegance, he was a down-and-out clutching at the last straws of dignity. He looked scornfully at the pair of us and laughed, making comments about our appearance. We were too cold and hungry to be angry as he spoke to us as if we were a couple of village idiots. An old green-haired woman laughed in great glee at his every comment. We ignored his questions which he put to us like a schoolmaster of an infants class. "A most uneducated clientele you get here, Flossie," he said to the stall-keeper. "I'll tell you what, answer me this one and I'll stand you both a cup of tea. If you had one shilling and sixpence in your left trouser pocket and half-a-crown in the right one, what would you have?"

"Someone else's trousers, mate," answered Knuttles and off we sauntered away from the shrieks of laughter blown back into the sniggerer's face.

The Cheshire side of Manchester's suburbia was a contrast both from the dinginess and feeling of despondency rife in the city, and the poor pickings for griddlers. It was also good for handout clothes and we called on as many large houses as possible to offer our services, oftener than not (to our relief) we were politely refused by the maid, on the instructions of the butler but given a hot drink and sometimes an article of the master's wardrobe. As this was Cotton-owners' territory, we picked up some good stuff. The pleasant flat lands of Cheshire are nice for summer bumming but the bigger places were the goals in the winter, so we headed for Chester, deciding to make it the parting of the ways. Johnny had other fish to fry, so he said, which I assumed meant he had some dodge up his sleeve which he could handle himself. Ours had been an amicable partnership and we meant to end it in a pub close to a canal on the outskirts of the town. As we walked along a lane the sounds of band music floated across from the opposite side of the canal. I recognised it immediately as a Salvation Army band for having hung idly around towns on Sunday evenings for many years I had often joined in with the singing, for many of the hymns were ones I knew from those innocent days as a chorister. Knuttles could have made a living as a mind-reader on the halls, and said "Before you burst into tears of remorse for your past life of sin, Joe, get behind the band and go round with the tin. They'll never know any difference." Now most bands performed in a circle, but these Salvationists had formed a straight line along a grass verge skirting the lane. An audience of several dozen people were standing close together on the opposite side of the lane, joining in the singing of 'Come All Ye Faithful'. Christmas was only a week away. Behind the band was another group of people holding Bibles but not wearing uniforms. It was to this group that Johnny directed me. The only bandsman who could have noticed me was the conductor who was facing the band and using his baton with great fervour, but his eyes were on the music. When the carol was over the conductor announced that as it was a cold night there wouldn't be the usual proclamation of faith by Sister Cecilia, instead the band broke into a spirited rendition of one of the old favourites and as the familiar strains inspired the Bible group into joyous singing I moved amongst them with the tin, at the same time augmenting the singing with my lusty baritone:

> *When upon life's billows you are tempest tossed,*
> *When you are discouraged, thinking all is lost,*
> *Count your many blessings, name them one by one,*
> *And it will surprise you what the Lord has done.*
>
> *Count your blessings one by one!*
> *Count your blessings, see what God has done!*
> *Count your blessings, name them one by one,*
> *And it will surprise you what the Lord has done!...*

By the sound of the rattling the tin was collecting a nice pile of coppers. 'There are tides in the affairs of men' some clever know-all once said, but what he didn't say was that there is also a time when a man must know when to quit. I walked up that bank, still chanting, and met my companion on the canal bank where we counted our blessings and the collection money as we drummed-up some tea and waited for the pub to open.

13

CHRISTMAS DAY IN THE DOSS-HOUSE

Visiting that pub was a lucky stroke for there we met Canal Charlie, a well-known pub singer who performed in canalside pubs for trippers. As Sunday singing was prohibited, Charlie was sponging drinks off the 'regulars' and not doing very well. He travelled the canal tow-paths following a unique form of livelihood for he seldom left the waterways, sleeping beneath bridges and making his home in boatsheds and on moored barges. The exception he made was at Chester where he always slept at Big Bessie's.

After the manner of all men on the tramp, we swapped yarns and experiences but, as Charlie only called at houses along the canal side, we knew it was no use asking him if he knew of any good 'marks': the water-side was his private beat and any man who knew Charlie respected the fact for he had a reputation for thumping a man first then warning him afterwards. Knuttles drank up and was ready for the off and Charlie was able to show him a short cut, along the tow-path, to the main road where he hoped to get a lift to try his luck in the South. Ours had been a congenial partnership yet I was still surprised when Knuttles presented me with a parting gift. He put a penny in a slot-machine from which he took two Woodbines and two matches. I'd put many hundred pennies in such machines before.

"Good luck, Joseph," said Johnny. "One day we might meet again."

And then he was gone, following some scent or other of which he had got wind. I felt sad really. I liked the man and couldn't really say as much for Canal Charlie, who was to be my mate for the evening. Though we were virtual paupers in Manchester, our financial resources had taken an upward turn and the collection had helped enormously.

Charlie was a morose sort of chap most times but now he was in a communicative frame of mind because he knew I was in funds. Seeing his chance, he invited me to spend Christmas Eve and Christmas Day in Bessie's place. Only too glad to accept, I treated Charlie to several pints. Tomorrow I'd be stony-broke, but that was the way of things and I never worried and Bessie's hospitality at Christmas was legendary to the boys on the pad. I had stayed there on odd occasions, but never at the festive season for she only invited her own favourites or special mates of Charlie's who, quite openly, lived with her in her private apartment when in Chester. I felt honoured, not only by the offer, but by a rare event. Lulled into nostalgia and, who knows what other emotions prompted his confidences, but I was to hear a fellow tramp's story — why he had become what he was. Novelists, journalists and film-makers sought such copy avidly, for it had appeal — the real story behind the rags. The little pride left prevented this with most tramps; they hated people who pried. And so the writers invented their own versions of life at the lower level and this is the reason why so much nonsense had been written about the tramp. But in that pub a tramp willingly told another the story of his particular fall. Only Charlie's real name has been changed for, even today, his name is familiar to some people who may remember him on the stage.

Charles Holbrook was born in Lincolnshire in 1880, the son of a clergyman of a tiny hamlet. The lad sang in the choir, his voice showing promise at a very early age. As he grew older he sang solo at Church concerts around the district. His father hoped he would follow him into the Ministry, but Charles dreamed of being an opera singer. His father's incumbency was poorly paid and the family, four more children in addition to Charles, took every available penny. There was no money to pay for the luxury of singing lessons. So he found work on a local newspaper as a reporter, paying for the odd lesson, from a local singer, out of his salary. Meeting people through his job, he was soon offered engagements for local concerts. The first fee was 5/-.

But that offer was the start of many family rows. His father adamantly refused to let him perform for money and considered that the other members on the Concert Bill were not the type of companions a vicar's son should be cultivating.

After several refusals and a serious row, Charles left home and found a room. He also found a mistress, a chorus girl from one of the concert parties he was singing with in the evenings. When the impoverished vicar found out that his son had fallen to such low depths he publicly condemned him from his own pulpit. This unprecedented action in the Church became a local scandal and was fanned into national flames by an eager young reporter — no less than the recalcitrant son himself who was now a free-lance journalist. When his father learned that Charles was making copy out of his own sinfulness he tracked him down to Cleethorpes, where he had a weekend engagement with a pierrot group on the beach, his mistress being a dancer with the same group. Pious fury knowing no bounds, the vicar forced his way into the changing-tent and confronted the girl with her sins whilst Charles was singing on the beach. So overcome with rage was the vicar that he struck the girl across her face with his cane. When Charles entered the tent he saw the girl, her face running with blood, and his father. So incensed was he that it took four other members of the cast to pull him off the vicar. The girl was scarred for life, left the party and Charles's life for ever. In that tent was born the demon which was to dog him for the rest of his life.

Despite his success in pierrot shows and smoking concerts as a tenor soloist, his uncontrollable temper was always the reason for him losing connections with Booking Agents. At the slightest whim he would row with musicians and other artists who were trying to further his career and, as a balm to the depressions which followed these outbursts, he took to the bottle. But his voice was good and despite his bad reputation for insulting accompanists and choir masters he was sort after by concert agents. As the years went by his need for drink grew stronger until he was unable to sing without the support of a half bottle of whisky inside him. Then the war came, but the drink had ruined his constitution. He could sing no more and as a soldier he was useless and eventually, on Army medical advice, was discharged. And then a minor miracle in the life of Charles Holbrook occurred. At the age of twenty nine, a fine voice ruined, a drunken sop, he was spotted by a former concert agent who now booked acts for after-dinner engagements and the third-rate music-hall circuit. His sister was the Matron of a Home for Alcoholics and Charles agreed to go for treatment to be 'dried out', with the promise of future work from the agent. The cure seemed miraculous at first, a wonderful transition took place and, what was most important, his voice regained its former quality and strength. The agent realised he had a property worth cultivating so straight away he booked him on the third-rate music-hall circuit, billing him as the 'Velvet-Voiced Linnet'.

With the war over, the music-halls were doing big business; the people were singing again and singers like Charles were popular. Besides, his voice had the quality to raise him up the ladder to the larger theatres and by 1920 he was touring with the elite of the profession. In modern parlance 'he had arrived' but, already, that vile temper had given him a notoriety amongst the theatricals far removed from the image he created on stage singing the love songs of the day. He assaulted stage-doormen, rowed with managers and, as the drink took over again, his arrogance and aggression became unbearable to fellow artists. Some even refused to share Bills with him and his outbursts of rage made regular copy in the papers as he left a trail of destruction in the dressing-rooms and managers' offices around the country. After only two years at the top he was out of work. Exactly two years after topping the Bill at one of Yorkshire's leading theatres, he was busking outside the same theatre with a band of other has-beens. His voice was still his livelihood and for a while he made enough at busking to keep him in drink, but then there was a violent row and his buddies left him, not being able to tolerate his temper any more.

So another man became a tramp. By some quirk of life's sorting system, he began travelling the canal paths finding that the waterside pubs were good places for a man to sing for his supper and sponge drink. The bargees took pity on him and gave him food and shelter. One day he ventured into Chester and met a kindred spirit, Big Bessie who kept a dosshouse. She had a piano which only she played and as soon as Charles heard her play he knew immediately that here was a fine musician. Bessie, like himself, had once been a prominent solo performer. Charles would sing to her accompaniment; they became lovers and any man who liked music was indeed fortunate to be staying at Bessie's when Canal Charlie was there. But his temper knew no bounds if she played a note which didn't please him — it was sufficient for a violent row to flare up. But back Charlie would go when next he was near Chester, two atoms of wasted talent drawn to each other by that unfathomable chemistry of human behaviour.

But Back to Christmas. Bessie brewed her own beer and put on a special brew for her guests at Christmas. She was a rough sort but kind-hearted and the guests were given a free Christmas — breakfast, dinner, entertainment and as much beer as they could drink. Her cellar was packed with casks and bottles of the brew and it was said that she drank ten pints a day.

Canal Charlie gave me a very good tip-off about a barge moored along the canal where a man could wheedle in amongst the cargo of barrels and sacks and rest comfortably under the thick tarpaulin covering. This sufficed until I moved into Bessie's place on Christmas Eve and I spent the few days on the mooch around Chester.

When I arrived at her place on Christmas Eve she welcomed me warmly. Like the perfect host, fires had been lit in the sleeping rooms and I felt fortunate to be ensconced in such a place at Christmas when other chaps would be on the streets unable to get somewhere to stay. Christmas Eve was strictly the feed-yourself routine, as normal, but the great day itself, according to my room-mates, would be a day to be remembered forever. The warmth of the room was conducive to sleep and the next morning we awoke to an appetising aroma of frying bacon and found the communal kitchen transformed into a gay, unrecognisable room. Apparantely the Sisters and Brothers of the Church Army had arrived after we had been packed off to bed early, like kids who needed sleep to make them ready for the feast in store. Traditional Christmas trappings festooned the walls, holly hung from the gas mantles and every crevice and outcrop of plaster in the once ornate ceiling. Coloured balls glittered and streamers criss-crossed the room, like tangled tram lines, in gay profusion. A huge table was set out for breakfast on which red candles in saucers blazed a friendly welcome. The girls of the Army were the waitresses. Large jugs of home-made ale stood in the middle of the table and I couldn't but marvel at the way the devoted Army girls ignored the quantities of beer we men drank, in preference to tea, a practice they had been brought up to abhor. Yet they accepted that such men like us did drink beer and they didn't let this deter them from their good work. I know of other religious bodies who would have been outraged at our behaviour.

Bessie's brew was potent and was in plentiful supply and her guests were soon in a festive mood. After a first-class breakfast out came the cards and we played Three-card Brag and Pontoon whilst the Sisters helped Bessie with the chores and the preparation of the dinner. At twelve o'clock Father Christmas entered, heralded by a trio of Church Army musicians. He gave us each a silver threepenny 'bit'. The old chap next to me cried unashamedly and told me that it was the best Christmas he had spent for more years than he cared to remember. And then the band struck up the well-loved carols and we all joined in with gusto. The beer had taken hold, but Bessie knew her guests, there were no trouble-makers or men who got nasty in drink. The tambourines rang and jingled and a real traditional Christmas party was being enjoyed. But Canal Charlie wasn't satisfied with the beer, he was lacing it with meths. I saw him and Bessie had seen him also. He was grumbling and muttering comments about the carols and the musicians. Then one of the 'soldiers' gave a short sermon on the true meaning of Christmas, stressing the charity shown by Bessie to men who had no homes of their own; he wasn't being patronising like so many preachers I had heard. There was a sincerity in the man, devoid of cant and pietism and he held the attention of every man in the room, except Charlie who was muttering derogatory remarks about 'buttery-mouthed Bible bashers,' for Charlie could never forget his father had been a parson. And as he could never forgive his father he, consequently, detested all religions whatever the Creed. Bessie's face revealed her feelings of acute embarrassment, but the Army men ignored Charlie and after the sermon one of the company requested a carol. Charlie rose to his feet unsteadily and thumped the table savagely.

"We'll have no more soddin' carols — I'll give you a song. These bleedin' Holy Joes can't sing — come on, Bessie, help me out on the piana — get off your arse, you old bag, and play for me — d'year me, missus, or are you deaf?"

One of the musicians was going to come to Bessie's aid, but she simply said, "I'll handle him. He's had too much to drink," and, summoning up great control, she sat at the piano. "Well, what's it to be, Charlie? Let's have a happy song everyone knows."

"What about 'Jingle Bells'?" suggested the accordian player.

"Bleedin' Jingle Bells? Who'd you think we are, mate, a bleedin' kindergarten class — no we'll have something the lads can join in proper — Christmas Day in the Workhouse — you can rattle your tambourine, Sister Anna, when we get to the chorus - - -."

Bessie was outraged. "You'll not sing that lewd song in front of these good Christian people, Charlie Holbrook. Get out of here or I'll call the police — d'you hear me — out!"

"Belt up, you stupid old bitch," shouted Charlie and struck Bessie, knocking her off the stool. "I'll play the soddin' thing meself. Right, lads, lift the roof on the chorus — one, two, three — —

> *It was Christmas Day in the Workhouse,*
> *The happiest day of the year.*
> *Men's hearts were full of gladness*
> *And their bellies full of beer.*
> *Then up strolled Private Shorthouse*
> *His face as bold as brass*
> *Saying, we don't want your Christmas pudding*
> *You can stick it up your - - - -*

Chorus

Tidings of comfort and joy!
Comfort and Joy!
Tidings of comfort and joy - - - - -

It was Christmas Day in the Harem
And the eunochs were hanging around
And hundreds of beautiful women
Were stretched out on the ground
When in strolled the bold, bad Sultan
And gazed on his marble halls
Saying, "What do you want for Christmas, boys?
And the eunochs answered - - - - -

Chorus

We sang four more verses in similar vein. I'm sure that every man in that room felt embarrassed at this offensive intrusion into the carol service, but we were full of beer and we were tramps, not monks, and so the rafters rang with the bawdy classic sung with a fervour that even exceeded that we had put into Good King Wenceslas. It stood to the credit of the Army folk that they simply left us to it and busied themselves helping with the dinner, laying the table and doing their best not to be offended.

The spirit of the feast of Christmas vanished with the dying words of the song. Dinner was eaten in silence. As for Charlie, he collapsed by the piano and Bessie needed no assistance to manhandle him to the front door where she pushed him into the street. One of the Brothers went to his help. Her Christmas was ruined. After the meal we were sent on our way accompanied by a string of curses – she could vent her anger now that the religious folk had gone. Her good nature had been trampled in the mud. Never again did she offer free hospitality at Christmas time.

With the comfortable knowledge that we had two good meals inside us, we took to the streets, off in different directions, disappointed men who were faced with the prospect of kipping out for the night with no chance of a room anywhere else on Christmas night.

During the following spring Charlie was found drowned in the Shropshire Union Canal. The one-time tenor voice had uttered one last note — a cry for help. But it was too late. The next day a short article appeared in a local paper. The reporter said he had known Charlie well and that he had sung for coppers on the Canal Bank and in the Pubs, being a well-known character to bargees and boat people. His last sentence intrigued me, however: "Having heard him sing, it was obvious that he was not the ordinary street busker type; had his life circumstances been different who knows but that he could have made a success of his chosen career." A fitting epitaph for the graves of many unknown wayfarers.

14

A WINTER'S TALE

Living rough in the spring and summer could be another form of paradise, but in the winter a taste of hell. It killed off hundreds of wandering folk every year. I know of many incidents where men were found frozen stiff. To sleep out in the winter was taking a great risk no matter how hardened a man was to the elements; weakness would cause unconsciousness and the frost would do the rest. The notorious Shap Fells in Westmorland were the death of many tramps, so bad were they that the local Kendal Toc H organised a tramp rescue service and regularly took men off the Fell to a comfortable room in Kendal. But such men were fools and courted death. At a very early stage I soon realised that if I was to live to a ripe old age — rare for tramps — I would have to take care of myself in the winter. So the doss-house stove became the centre of my desires, the kitchens were hot and the sensible man made sure he got into one as early in the evening as possible to stake his claim by the fire. It was the focal point and the tramp's whole being was ruled by it, the life of the house revolved around it.

Now take your average tramp and strip him. You would have found it a laborious job for he had more skins on him than an onion. He rarely refused clothes if they were offered so that a gift of a pair of trousers would be worn on top of the existing pair, and with other articles of clothing it would be the same — pile upon pile. In the summer time he sold them to Old Clothes Shops, but when the cold season came he wore all the clothes he could accumulate. The sharp onset of frost would often promote hand-outs and I once received three pairs of trousers in a week, one pair having graced the legs of a Banker, one a Vicar and the third from an Undertaker. This triple alliance of banking, bibles and burying kept my lower parts well protected against a particularly savage winter. Newspaper is a great body insulator and very necessary to the man who has to sleep rough on occasions. For there were times when the kip-rooms would be full to overflowing, or you were stuck between towns and had to find a shed or a barn or huddle into the recess of a railway tunnel or whatever. Sheets of newspaper have saved many a man's life.

The sensible tramp didn't bath or wash in the winter months for the dirt helped to keep him warm whereas the man on the spike circuit was forced to bath by Law, which was going to the other extreme, but I preferred the freedom of sleeping where I desired and put up with the dirt. This particular animal believed in keeping itself warm in the winter and bathing plenty in streams and lakes during the warmer months to make up for it.

'Massa' Bendigo was the nickname of a black tramp — a 'Shiny' as negroes were known colloquially. They were a very rare species and I only met one other, genuine one that is, for one bitter morning poor old 'Massa' was found as stiff as a ramrod in a ditch in Doncaster. Somehow he survived and pulled through the ordeal at the local infirmary, where he was subjected to hot baths over a continual period of time. When he went back on the pad he was no longer a 'negro' — Massa had been so black with dirt he had deceived everyone. Being naturally brown-skinned, he soon adopted the caste of a negro once again and the name Massa stuck, white man or not.

Consequently, the lodging-houses did far more trade at this time of year and I often saw men fighting to get a place in the queue at the deputy's window. This gathering of the clans gave me time to study my fellow man and learn the tricks of the trade, for in the average house all manner of riff-raff and tricksters would be gathered together, a cross-section of roguery and the seamier side of life. Genuine tramps were in the minority in these places. The outright beggar was a sickening creature, having no sense of cunning or any degree of plausibility whatsoever. The Public detested him, yet he made them feel ashamed by his downright adoption of unashamed alms seeking; they knew that many of them were rogues yet they could never really convince themselves that he was not a deserving case. So, in this way many people paid to salve their conscience. I played many roles in my time, some innocent enough, like genuine work, others fraudulent, but I never begged though I admit that button and elastic selling was only a step above it, simply a sophisticated form of begging.

There were many types of beggars, some more sickening than others. Particularly loathsome were those who wrapped their limbs in filthy bandages and sported these as 'war wounds' on doorsteps. Others borrowed a young child from its mother and stood with it in the gutter, the better to wring the pity of the passerby. The forged letter trick was a great favourite with this type and he was never without a letter in his pocket which had been written by his Commanding Officer, no less! 'This is to certify that John Aloysious Jones was a stout honest man who served his country well in its hour of need . . .' He appealed to all to support the aforementioned John Aloysious Jones in *his* hour of need. As in all crookery there existed the behind-the-scenes brigade, the providers and the fences — in this case the man in the doss-house who wrote in a good hand and could pen a letter purporting to have been written by an educated man, such as an officer. A provider I knew in Manchester turned these letters out at a shilling a time — an extortionate amount then, but he knew that the beggar could afford to pay him and couldn't purchase a better bogus letter from anyone else. Besides, his living depended on it. This type of provider would turn his hand to all sorts of letter-writing, producing any recital of falsehoods the customer requested; or perhaps his chief business would be writing begging letters which he sent through the post. For instance, Jemmy Spiker specialised in Society Births, Deaths and Marriages, this information being provided in the more upper-class newspapers which he either scrounged or was forced to scan at the local library. To the lady and gentleman who had been blessed by the arrival of an heir he would compose a missive of congratulation but always adding a postscript of how he had once been a proud father . . . but alas and alack! . . . Cruel fate! You can imagine the list of misfortunes an accomplished sponger like Jemmy could spin. To the relatives of a deceased person went a letter of profound sympathy, to a newly married couple a letter of congratulations and sincere wishes for a blissful life – oh! how the pen of Jemmy Spiker poured forth the heartbreak of a man once happily married until disaster struck; and how, in the hour of their joy, a few inconsequential shillings would restore a vestige of comfort to a poor struggling man down on his luck through no fault of his own. I swear I once saw him weep as he wrote a letter. If a colonel had buried his mother then Jemmy had been a proud member of his regiment. Jemmy had a story for every occasion and made a good living, working on the law of averages, always requesting that all 'loans' should be sent to him c/o Poste Restante for, he told them, he could never stand the shame of his relatives finding out that he was accepting charity. He would plan his route well in advance and call at the post office in each town he passed through. Such a hoaxer had to keep on the move for the police were constantly weeding-out his kind. In a lodging-house in Wigan he showed me a wallet packed with postal orders. The begging letter game was well worth all the effort.

Little Binky Bones had a great graft going for him until he was tracked down by the police and forced back to his old trade of selling flower 'buttonholes' outside the Midland Hotel in Manchester. Binky advertised in newspapers: 'Make yourself a good living – send five shillings for amazing details'. Even at that price he caught plenty of suckers. In reply they received a printed slip of paper which read – 'Do as I do!' Simplicity, the essence of deception. Strictly speaking there was no crime committed. He could have argued forcibly that he was telling the truth. It never came to that. Binky was warned off by the police and did as he was told but not before he had amassed a nice little pile of money.

But though I detested out and out begging, I was not fool enough or proud enough to refuse a hand-out given freely. One cold winter's day in Chester I was standing on a corner with an Irishman known as Myles O'Toole. Many tramps were known by nick names and he was somewhat irreverently dubbed 'Yards O'Cock'. Like a lot of his race he was never without a grin on his face and a ready answer on his lips. Keeping company with Yards was a pleasure for he was full of jokes and he never moaned like a lot of the chaps I met. Yards was down because of his own fault and he admitted it. He had let the family farm fall into disrepair through his fondness for drink. One night he came home from the pub blind drunk, lit a cigarette and fell asleep. The old homestead back in the County Cork was destroyed. His sister could never forgive him so out he set on the road with what was left in the ruins, a few bits and pieces which fitted into a sack, and had never seen his sister since. Though he bitterly regretted what he had done he couldn't go back to the new home his sister had found, so he wandered, lived on his wits until he grew to like the life. When I met him he was a seasoned man of the road and the happiest one I ever met. Apart from his unique name, his claim to fame was that he had once spent a summer on a very profitable coup, namely selling autographed photographs of St. Patrick to American pilgrims to the Mountain of Croagh Patrick where the saint is said to have prayed and fasted. But the gag became too popular and other artful dodgers moved in to ruin the pitch. They always do.

That day in Chester was a freezer and Yards kept muttering comments about brass monkeys as we stamped our feet trying to keep warm waiting for the doss-house to open its doors. A well-dressed chap was eyeing us with a strange sort of curiosity, the sort of man who gave a lesser mortal a coin because it made him feel important. I knew human nature by experience and had diagnosed this character in a flash but I never possessed Yards' ready wit. The fellow looked at us with condescension, handing us a penny each and saying, "it's not charity. I only do it because it amuses me." Quick as a flash Yards retorted. "Then why don't yiz make it half-a-dollar apiece and have yizelf a bloody good laugh!"

Like most of his countrymen, he was a great lover of bloodstock and every day he would scour the papers, picking out 'winners', that is, until one day in Ludlow he met an old acquaintance. Having nothing else to occupy myself, I'd travelled with him for he was good company and his knowledge of road-lore beneficial. We were kipping in brick kilns most nights on our journey, a means of keeping warm I'd never tried before, and were probably warmer lying on the straw than guests in the best hotels nearby. The fire during the day ensured that the kilns were still hot at night, and most brick firms let tramps doss in them, provided they did no harm. After a long slog from Leominster, I was making a meal in a kiln when Yards appeared obviously on the best side of a few pints and singing at the top of his voice. We ate the bacon I'd cooked between us then Yards took me to a back street pub to meet his pal, Reggy, an old cell mate from Wakefield Prison. Reggy was a horsey man of the cheap, brash variety; the fourth-rate bookie's clerk type, definitely not to be trusted, a ferrety look on a weasel face, craftiness in its every line proclaiming he was a man who lived on his wits and other people's stupidity. Skulduggery on race courses takes all forms, but Reggy operated outside the course, catching the punter before he paid his entrance money, which means the pubs adjacent to the course. Over a slow burning cigar apiece, supplied by Reggy, he explained his technique, for Yards had told him that I was game for any little plan he might have in mind. I was an eager listener.

"I live well, Mate," he told me. "You stick with me and Yards here and you'll be smoking cigars every night. But first you'll need smartening up see, not too much mind, just enough to make you look a bit shabby but definitely respectable. You're a stable lad see. That beard comes off for a start. Don't worry, Mate, on the brass you'll be making you'll soon buy a neckerchief to keep your neck warm. I want you to sit in this same boozer tomorrow at twelve o'clock see, no later 'cause me and Yards have to make hay while the suckers are biting. Here's a bob for your beer money and half-a-crown to get yourself togged out at a Jumble Sale. Sup and get off to the one at the church-hall down the street. They'll be finishing soon and they'll let you have the leftovers for a song. Keep the change, Mate

— here twelve on the dot pronto and all you have to say when the geezer hands you a tip is 'Thanks, guvner!' Nothing else. Got it? See you, Mate!"

The temptation to do a bunk was uppermost in my mind. I had a whole half-crown to spend on drink, but I was bound to run into Yards again so I headed for the church-hall, being careful to nip my cigar before entering. An Havana-smoking tramp might have caused suspicion amongst the ladies of the Mothers' Union. But as it was they were the essence of kindness and sorted out a variety of garments and a pair of boots to make me look more presentable as they had done for Yards earlier. I even picked up a razor and the whole lot only cost me a shilling. So, with the aid of a piece of soap appropriated from the gentlemen's lavatory, I set out for another pub. Here I did a quick change in the lavatory, making sure to keep on the layers of good thick Fleet Street paper round my legs, then went to a public lavatory where I invested a half-penny for a wash and shave. Five minutes with the cut-throat and the tramp had vanished. Before me in the brown-cracked mirror, I saw an unfamiliar reflection — that of a tall sunburnt man wearing a faded multi-patched purple velveteen smoking jacket over a green pullover and a white tie. A pair of mildewed but thick brown tweed plus-fours and scuffed black shoes completed my somewhat discordant ensemble. As I left the public lavatory the attendant said, "You with a stable, mate?" I nodded and hurried on before he could ask me for a tip for tomorrow's meeting. Back at the first pub Reggy and Yards were still drinking and the only occupants of the snug room. I sat down at a table with a half of mild. My appearance in the room only attracted cursory glances until Reggy asked casually, "You at the races tomorrow, mate?"

"Yes," I replied. "I'm working a fly trick with two other reprobates, one's an Irishman bearing the baptized name of Myles O'Toole."

Momentarily they were speechless . . . "Jaysus, it's yizelf!" said Yards at last.

Reggy did a double swallow in amazement. "And here was me thinking you was a likely sucker. Bleedin' creepers, mate, you look the part to a tee. Stone me, mate, but I wouldn't have known yer. Here's your bob, Yards, me old mate, he's turned up like you said he would. Get the ale in with this, Joe, and we'll drink to the start of what I reckon's going to be a very happy little business association."

Back at the brick kiln Yards told me Reggy had bet him a shilling that I wouldn't return after he'd given me the half-crown for the jumble clothes. It seems that he had told him I was to be trusted, a tramp I might be but a man who wouldn't double-cross his own sort. He had recognised the camaraderie of the road in my make-up. To which Reggy had replied, "Balls! He'll run off, scarper. You'll see."

Yards was delighted I hadn't flown and he'd won a shilling, and we were in business for the races the following day. Next day as the clock struck twelve o'clock I was seated in the snug room, awaiting the results of the oracle being worked on an unsuspecting victim at that very moment. It was an old trick but a good one, and still worked today. Reggy would take the lead as they idled in a nearby bar with eyes alert for the right sucker. Selecting one, Reggy would then sidle up to him, grab him by the shoulder and exclaim, "Well, what d'you know? How are you, mate?" The victim had to shake his hand, of course, as Reggy exuded surprised delight. "Fancy meeting you again — let's see, was it Chester? No? - - - Liverpool? — I've got it, Haydock Park — well, well — it's a small world, mate. Keeping well are you, mate? That was a great tip you gave me — remember? A belter, I backed it on the snout I did, six to one. Come on, mate, I'll get 'em in. Come and join me and the mate over there." The victim never has a chance to say a word until he is seated at the table, where he is bombarded with more vocal blandishments. "What a tip, mate! It was good of you, mate, real good; kind — wasn't it kind, Yards? This chap — I've forgotten your name, mate, sorry —"

"Charlie," the victim managed to say.

"Charlie, of course! Fancy me forgetting. Well, Charlie and me met at Haydock once — *was* it Haydock, Charlie?"

"I don't honestly — er — remember," says Charlie in a state of embarrassed confusion.

"No, it wasn't Haydock! I've got it — Bangor on Dee, that's it! Course it was. Good old Bangor over the Sticks."

"But I've never —" begins Charlie.

"Sup up, mate. Here get Charlie another half, Yards me old pal — no, the drinks is on me, Charlie, I insist — well well — now I knows a pal when I sees one and I don't forget. I mean I won sixteen oncers on your tip. No, mate, I can't let that pass — here." He winks and Charlie moves over closer for the imparting of secret information. Reggy modulates his voice to a whisper of intrigue. "Can't be too careful, mate; lot of rogues get in here on race days." Charlie nods in agreement, Reggy narrows his already narrow eyebrows and urges Charlie even closer with a flick of his head. "Brown Bazil, two o'clock. Cinch," nodding his head adamantly three times. "Past the post, mate." Looks around carefully, puts finger on lips. "Keep it quiet though, only I know something, see."

Charlie nods out of admiration. He is already on the hook. When Yards returns he is brought in as the vote of confidence to the resolution that Brown Bazil will win in a canter in the two o'clock.

"Cinch," says Yards as if the very suggestion of it doing anything else would be ludicrous. "I thought we wus going to keep it between us though, Reggy." Yards doesn't disguise the disappointment in his voice.

"We are, mate, but Charlie here put me on a winner and I'm giving him one now, but button it, Charlie me old sparrow, it's a wow, see? Thirtyfives — can't lose. I'm in with the lads, see?"

"Gosh! That's a price! Thirtyfive to one!"whistles Charlie. "I'll put half a quid on that."

"Half a quid!" exclaim our two tipsters in unison. "No, mate, think big. This is a chance of a lifetime — well between you and me, Charlie, it's from the horse's mouth — well, the stable lads anyway — they've saved it, see? Put your shirt on it, mate. Well come on, drink up and I'll take you to meet the stable lad — he's in the King's Head yonder. I always give him a fiver for himself — I mean, what's a fiver when I'm going to win a fortune. Peanuts, I say."

"Peanuts!" echoes Charlie, laughing. "Always grease the works well, hey?" And the rich-man-to-be follows Reggy and Yards to the snug where I am nursing half a pint of ale waiting to mutter the immortal words. Reggy greets me, thrusts a piece of paper in my hand, saying, "Got to make it snappy, Joe. Thanks, mate. I'll not forget this." Charlie follows suit and I feel a handful of *real* paper, a lovely crisp handkerchief-sized fiver. "Thanks, guvner," I says, as per the script and off they go their respective ways, Charlie to put all his savings on a horse that hasn't a snowballs chance in Hades and Reggy and Yards to pick out another mug.

That winter was the worst I've known for cold, but not for snow fortunately and the racing calendar wasn't too badly affected. Me and Yards followed Reggy around the circuit – Hereford, Chepstow, Cheltenham, Northampton, Beverley and Doncaster, to name but some of the courses – thumbing lifts on wagons and living very comfortably in lodging houses a good cut above the ones us two tramps were accustomed to; there was money to spare for booze, cigarettes and Reggy disappeared most nights to a local brothel. I was too frightened of getting a dose of the clap to follow suit, having seen what it did to men, and Yards made his excuse with typical wit saying that going with women was a sin and him being a good Catholic they were forbidden fruit. So the two of us would dull the temptations of the flesh which the accumulation of unaccustomed money fostered by spending our ill-gotten gains on drink. For three months we followed the horses, working the trick, Reggy taking half the rake-off and Yards and me sharing the other half; but knavery has a way of going stale all of a sudden. At Chester – back where I first met Yards – one of the cozened punters recognised Reggy and reported him to a policeman. He had placed twentyfive pounds on a horse that had run last out of fifteen starters. Reggy wasn't unknown to the police and so our benefactor was taken from us but, being the little fish, we slipped through the net to live another day. Reggy served his sentence and returned to the circuit only to be eventually found in an alley beaten up by a gang of race sharks he'd double-crossed. Another spell of good living was over, but I was too hardened to the harsh realities of life to have thought it would last for ever.

I parted company with Yards regretfully for we'd had

good times but were not a penny better off after it all. John Barleycorn had swallowed the lot. It was always my pattern to drink when I could afford it and forget about it when the coffers were empty; good fortune and a dread of the stuff, kept me off meths. Many tramps were meths drinkers and, once hooked, drank themselves to death, clamouring for it like wild beasts, the craving so fierce they would do anything to obtain it. A couple of pulls with a cup of water was enough to turn a man into a drunken moron. I took heed and never once did the spirit touch my lips.

So it was back to reality and the trudge round towns trying to keep warm, earn a few coppers, cadge, cajole or steal something to eat. Some days there would be nothing over for an indoor kip, here the intricate knowledge of the road paid dividends for I knew the warm spots — greenhouses that weren't locked at night, foundries and steel works where there were crannies and hidey-holes to bunk-up in for the night; railway stations were useful, too, but not as warm: but the brick kiln was the best of all. It was the first-come-first-served principle for there were many minds with the same purpose. During the days the libraries were the gathering places for the flotsam. Sometimes the genuine readers couldn't get near the papers for recumbent bodies. Libraries were warm and the tramp was drawn to heat. A favourite trick was to select a book, sit down with it at a table, then lean on the table and go to sleep. I've slept many an hour like this and been able to use the night for travelling to another town. But all my library visits were not for the purpose of a crafty siesta. My gluttony for knowledge, fostered by my practical interest in nature, gave me a real purpose to life; a man needs this whether he be king, general or tramp. I rarely read novels but devoured pages of biography, volume upon volume of encyclopedias and reference books, the knowledge I had gleaned during spring and winter about the flora and fauna of the countryside and the ways of birds and animals was consummated in the library during the cold season. Given a sprinkling of intelligent, well-read lodgers an evening in a doss-house could sometimes reach an intellectual plane. It is a fallacy to assume that most tramps were recruited from the lowest classes.

Though my literary bent was for non-fiction, I became captivated by Cervante's *Don Quixote*; the adventures of the shatterpated Spanish knight were taking up the daylight hours of an English knight of the road which he could ill-afford when hard-pressed to scrape a few coppers together during the limited light of a foggy November. Being of no fixed abode, I couldn't obtain a library ticket so I decided on the only other means of removing the book. I simply stuck it inside my coat and walked out of Bolton library. Three days later I finished the book only to find that I had read only the first volume. Now my appetite having been whetted by the first half, the thought of another volume lying on the library shelf was too tempting to resist, so I was on the steps at opening time and entered the lending room and removed Volume 2. Having the complete edition enabled me to consult back to the first book whilst reading the second one, this task taking me a full three weeks as I progressed northwards in vile weather. At the end of this time I was in Carlisle and had entered into the very soul and heart of the Knight of La Mancha and his valet, Sancho Panca. Here a peculiar sense of guilt engulfed me which was impossible to shake off. My intention had been to sell the books at a second-hand dealer's in the town, but a conscience can be a great nuisance to a man at times. It seemed a culpable act to deny some reader, a schoolchild maybe, the chance of enjoying the delights of a literary masterpiece free from a public library. For once I felt despicable, an emotion which hadn't troubled my conscience after my other petty felonies; so I made the matter right with myself and the Libraries by depositing both volumes on the lending shelf in Carlisle, inserting a bookmark with the words 'For return to Bolton, Lancs., Library' printed in large letters. I had no compunction, however, in removing a copy of 'British Birds,' which I still have.

A man shackled by the chores of marriage was to be pitied, so ran my philosophy on the road; a warm fire against the cold he may have but I had the *carte blanche* of life and high on the list of luxuries I placed the time available to me for reading and studying books. That novel kept me warm inside and lit up my mind in the way only a book can do. For weeks after reading it I travelled the wild regions of Spain with Don Quixote and Sancho Panca, reciting aloud favourite passages I had committed to memory, particularly snatches from Panca's letter to his master: 'I am so taken up with business that I have not the time to scratch my head or pare my nails, which is the reason they are so long. God help me! I tell you this, dear Master of mine, that you may not marvel, why I have not yet let you know whether it goes well or ill with me in this same Government, where I am more hunger-starved than when you and I wandered through woods and wildernesses.' I had empathy with the character and with the author who conveyed by his pen the tragi-comedy of life through the fantasies of a mad man. The Don Quixotes of the road were not clad in shining armour, but in rags and tatters without a Miguel de Cervantes to immortalise them for posterity and for future tramps to steal from library shelves. After discussing the book with another literary fancier over a bowl of steaming hot soup in a Church Army hut on the Great North Road, we sang four verses of *Nearer my God to Thee* as our part of the bargain, flapping our arms in time with the tambourines like penguins, keeping the circulation moving. After the hymn he tore a page from a hymn book and wrote the names of three books he recommended me to steal. They were Conan Doyle's *The White Company,* Victor Hugo's *Les Miserables* and Melville's *Moby Dick.* In Pontefract Library I chose the latter and settled down beside the hot pipes to take to sea with the mad captain, Ahab. We had hardly left the quayside on the mammoth voyage in quest of the great white whale when the caretaker announced closing time. I simply stove it into my sack and finished the great masterpiece off gradually whenever I could find a warm place to settle down for a read. I returned this one to Hull library, a much more suitable abode for a seafaring book than the grimy town of Pontefract, I thought. Infatuated by these great novels, I took the literary tramp's advice and stole *The White Company* and *Les Miserables;* I tramped to the French wars with Samkin Aylward, Hordle John, and Alleyne Edricson, not caring a jot for the snowdrifts and the ice I was battling against in reality — a good book banishes the harassments of life, and when that was finished I survived the horrors of the galleys with Victor Hugo's *Jean Lejean*, escaped, sweated blood and died a thousand deaths with him as he fought to preserve his freedom against the insane obsession of his former galley master. Those books kept me alive in spirit during a cruel winter.

The incident of petty crime was far greater in the wintertime amongst the rootless society. Many of them made no secret of the fact that December would see them in prison. A favourite trick was to throw a brick through a window, a jeweller's shop being the favourite choice for a longer sentence was attached, so provided you didn't purloin a string of pearls or a gold watch the sentence would just about cover the winter months. With some tramps it was an annual occurrence but I loved my freedom too much to willingly forfeit it. But such was the ludicrous state of affairs ordained by the Government that permitted a gaol to offer far better conditions to a man or woman than the casual ward of the workhouse. In this case crime did pay and the law of the land condoned it.

It is interesting to compare conditions in the two institutions. I have already described those which existed in casual wards and the laborious tasks which had to be fulfilled, but in prison a man could read, take exercise and eat and sleep in a clean cell. A man taken in overnight at a police station for a vagrancy offence was often the recipient of a good hot meal and a bed. It follows then that the defendant who pleaded 'not guilty' could have his trial held at a Quarter Sessions. During the waiting period he was virtually a guest of His Majesty, lapping up the heat and the rest, enjoying the food and laughing up his sleeve at the 'honest fools' in the spike facing the elements daily. The spike diet was frugal. Breakfast: Bread, margarine or dripping (1 oz.), Tea or skilly (watery gruel) or cocoa (1 pt.). This was repeated for supper except that an extra 2 oz. of bread was supplied. While the man in prison was eating **bacon**, bread and tea (plenty of it) for breakfast and a diet during the rest of the day including fresh meat, potatoes and vegetables, puddings and tea and cocoa. It mattered little whether a man was awaiting trial or serving a sentence, he was faring far better than if he was seeking shelter in casual wards.

The winter's tale of the doss-house was a wretched one. I saw life at its lowest, living in brothels, given shelter by harlots and 'madames', stood cheek by jowl with the wrecks of life — the 'queers', dregs of the underworld, perverts, coppers' narks and creeps of all ilks; the genuine tramp detested them but he had no option but to seek their company in the vile weather of an English winter. He was the falcon caged into subjection, but the spirit of man is resilient and, with patience, the cage would be opened and back he would go to the wild places of his understanding, the hills and lanes of his fond meanderings. Each year when winter gave way to spring, I felt like sending up a prayer of thanksgiving but the words would stick in my throat. I wasn't proud of my standing in life. I simply said a silent 'thank you' that I possessed the urge in my soul to want to leave the midden-society of towns, to feel the wind in my face on the moors, smell the green grass, watch new leaves buffeted on the eddies of gliding streams and hear the buzz of insects and the chatter of animals welcoming the season of bountiful plenty.

15

TERMINUS

Throughout the history of Man there have been wars and the rumour of wars. As the 'thirties ran their course, towards the end of the decade the name Adolf Hitler became more and more familiar to the people of Britain. Then, almost before this country realised it, he had become such a menace that we had no alternative but to go to war against Germany for the second time in my memory. To me he was almost a mythical figure and my world wasn't going to change because of a strutting maniacal Hun. I had great faith in the British Bulldog, despite my tramp hatred of the 'System'. I was on the other side of the fence, an untouchable – or so I thought.

On September 3rd 1939 war was declared. My little world changed from the moment Neville Chamberlain finished his historic speech; people spoke of nothing else, it was impossible to escape the stunning effect of the announcement of a second war.

As the months rolled by, tens of thousands of men were conscripted and when the authorities began to look into the loopholes of the system the vagrant population became a subject for scrutiny. I remember a scathing letter in the *Manchester Guardian* stating that thousands of men were roaming the country as tramps, dodging the column, whilst decent respectable young men were compelled to go to war. It was a letter which made great effect, others followed in different papers and the attitude of people towards us altered quite dramatically as a result. I knew that in the eyes of the public I, too, was dodging the column. Unrepentant, I went about my business though tending to sleep out more and more, for the doss-houses were subjected to spot checks by the police. They were not just looking for tramps but men living rough to avoid call-up, a new breed of tramps and, though most were rounded up, some did avoid arrest and had to tramp for the duration of the war, some never leaving the life even when it was all over. There was no brand of patriotism burning brightly in my breast either. One day, I heard a whisper that a couple of the lads had gone over to Ireland and I made up my mind to follow them. Life was getting hard. "You're old enough to fight, you are! Clear off and join the Services, or are you a coward?" This was said to me by a woman who, only a month earlier, had given me a roof over my head and a hot supper. Suspicion was in every crevice of every doss-house, in every library, darting from the eyes of passers-by along every street. It was very easy for the authorities to inspect vagrant wards for these were government institutions, but more difficult in doss-houses, but I took no chances and kept away from both as conscription activity increased with the passing of a National Service Act, which pushed the age of conscription up to forty-one, my age in those early months of 1940. Liability to register was placed on the individual and proclamations were displayed on prominent sites and everyone should have been aware of them and the dates of registration.

It is interesting to look back to those early war years and consider the attitude of the country towards vagrants. There was a special procedure for following up a man who failed to carry out his obligations under the National Service Acts because he was:

Normally of no fixed address

or

Deliberately moving from place to place in order to evade service.

The procedure was designed to ensure the registration of any such man who appeared liable under the Acts, but who had not already registered, and for his immediate attendance for medical examination if he had not already been examined. Anyone who had been medically examined was issued with a certificate of medical examination-card NS54 (Grade IV) or NS55 (Grades I to III).

The police were often instrumental in finding men who

could not produce their registration card NS2 and the local offices of the Ministry of Labour then interviewed the man. If he refused to register, although apparently liable, he was questioned as to his reasons and these were recorded and he was then instructed to attend for medical examination and grading. A notice (NS6) was issued to him stating when he should attend, even if he protested that his movements were too uncertain to enable him to be sure of attending on the date arranged. A report was made to the Allocation Local Office of the action taken. In some cases the man was escorted to the medical board by the police. If he did not attend for medical examination he could be prosecuted and subsequently jailed.

England was no longer an attraction. Even if I failed the medical examinations life could never be the same. They would find some kind of work for me. Gradually, I was heading for Liverpool, dossing down in whatever shelter I could find during the day and walking at night. When I was within a few miles of Liverpool I made a fire and cooked a meal by the side of the road. There was very little traffic on it and I felt safe enough. Then there was a sound which, at first, I took for thunder. It grew louder, more metallic, like no other sound I had heard, and suddenly the noise made sense to me – the tramp, tramp, tramp of marching feet. The first column of soldiers came into sight and I had a private viewing of a Regiment going to war. It was no use running away, I was wary only of police – not the military. I knew they wouldn't bother about a scruffy tramp. My appearance did attract comments though, for I represented freedom. I can never forget the looks of envy on those faces; kids' faces, some of them mere lads going to embark for duty in a foreign land, some giving up glorious futures, others leaving loved ones and the comfort of home and all carrying with them the uncertainty of ever returning. They were shattered men – stunned, saddened; yet they sang! It was still a 'Long Way to Tipperary'. They didn't know that I was far more likely to see Tipperary than they were. That very night I hoped to be on the sea, bound for Ireland, whilst they were bound for God knows where. "Lucky swine! Go on, mate, give us a swig of tea." "I envy you, mate!" "There'll always be a bloody England while you're here, mate!" Remarks like this came fast and furious. I suppose I must have represented the essence of pure contentment, and I laughed in their faces. I was a symbol of the England they were leaving behind, a familiar sight — merely a scruffy tramp brewing tea — but a symbol just the same and still I laughed at them. They were mugs. Young mugs. As the sound of booted feet died away I chuckled to myself and drank my tea.

Darkness was closing in fast as I skulked along the quays, an eye open for the chance to scuttle over the side of the steerage of the M.V. Leinster. I knew men who travelled to Ireland this way. They told me it was easy, simply a matter of biding time until the dockers were having a cup of tea and a fag. At the opportune moment I took my chance, dashing for the ship and the unwatched gangplank. It seemed so easy. It was, for the two huge policemen who closed in on me from the shadows of a tall crane.

"Don't tell me we've another after a free trip, Albert?" They laughed and took me to a police office on the quayside. These were Dock Police. Shortly, two city policemen arrived and I was taken by car to a hospital. There I was compelled to have a bath whilst one of the coppers waited outside the bathroom. Clad in a nightshirt, which reached down to my toes, I drank tea in an office and felt humiliated. They were laughing at me. And then my hair was cut and then a nurse led me back again to a huge slop-stone where she massaged my head fiercely with a foul-smelling black substance. When my hair was dry I was given a mirror to view my new image. By this time a couple of nurses had joined in the fun with the coppers. "He looked seventy-two when we picked him up, now he's only twenty-six," said one and the other laughed. I was then put to bed, like a scolded child, on a hard mattress. "Tomorrow, mate, you're going to join the bloody Army." There was no fun in the policeman's remark. I was well and truly caught.

In the morning, after a mug of tea and a round of toast, I was taken in a van to a Medical Centre somewhere in the city. I was warned that lying to questions would be looked on as a criminal act. So the alternative to enlistment was prison. The thought of prison made me decide to tell the truth. When my particulars were recorded on a form I was led into a red-tiled corridor which reaked of disinfectant; down the sides were long wooden forms, crammed with well-scrubbed, well-shorn, vagrancy clad in workhouse-type overalls. This was the waiting-room for the Medical Officer. That two-hour wait was the killer of my spirit. I was crushed and such was my detestation of enlistment that I was jealous of the weasel-faced chap next to me with the racking cough; envied the long gangling chap with the wheezing chest — wrecks who would return to what they really were, down and outs, life's cast-offs, doomed. I longed with a savage fervour to change my rude health for the diseases these men carried inside them. No man has detested his pending fate more than I did as I waited in that cold bare corridor.

"Next! Stacey." I felt like a man of lead as I walked the few short steps to the door.

The doctor read my report then proceeded to do all the repugnant things doctors do at Army Medicals. When the examination was completed he laughed. "No fixed abode, hey? A tramp?"

"Yes," I muttered.

"You'll call the Doctor 'Sir'!" The voice of a stiff, bristly sergeant tore at my eardrums. I shuddered, sick at heart.

"Yes, sir."

"Well, for forty-one you're a fit man by any standards. Been of no fixed abode for twenty years? Sergeant, do you realise this man is the fittest vagrant I've ever examined? Must be the fittest tramp in England. That's something, what? He's yours now, sergeant."

"Sir!"

I was in that strange state between laughter and tears, perched on the razor-thin edge between both. As I got dressed I started to laugh, stirred by the comical irony of the situation. Here I was, a reject of society, dragged back by that same society to help fight its oppressors. I would be compelled to follow rules I had long since disregarded, a reluctant cog in the wheel of war; the fittest tramp in England! I saw the sick joke and laughed until my belly ached and then I felt I wanted to weep. But I couldn't.

Military bull-shit was drummed into me at some camp on the Welsh borders, near Oswestry I believe. Route marches, cross-country running, endless drill — and I took to it like a trained athlete. I was uniformed, blancoed and bawled at unmercifully — six weeks later I was a trained soldier. My mates all left for the Front. I was left behind. It seemed that, due to my age, the army couldn't quite make up its mind about Private Stacey. Then I was summoned to attend for interview with an officer.

"Your age is against active service, Stacey. Seems once you were a clerk in civvy street — some while ago though."

"Yes, sir."

"Well, I've got some news for you, Private." He rustled some papers in a filing cabinet. Did it contain my release papers? Suddenly I realised I was a tramp no more. I had crossed the great divide and didn't want to go back. Here was another ironic situation for you. And yet I think it was bettered by what the officer told me. "It seems, Private Stacey, that you have been rejected for active service. You have been seconded to the Pay Corps." A smile played around his lips and he turned back to the cabinet to hide it. I believe he wanted to laugh.